Keep on Laughing

John C. Walker

Printed by:
A & J Printing
P.O. Box 518
Nixa, MO 65714

Published by: J.A.W.'s Publishing
Order from:
John A. Walker
530 Alger Ave.
Manistique, MI 49854
Phone: 906-341-2082

Library of Congress Cataloging-In-Publication Data
Walker, John A.

ISBN 0-9639798-3-3

2nd Printing

John A. Walker writes for:
White Pine Publishing Inc.
212 Walnut St.
Manistique, MI 49854
Phone: 906-341-5200
(Manistique Pioneer Tribune)

These stories are written to show the humorous side of working as a Game Warden - living in Michigan U.P. They are not meant to offend anyone and are just the writers version of the stories as he heard or saw them. No names are used in the stories without prior approval.

Dedicated To:

Erine Skinner, Billy Lundberg, Kenny Somero

Three school friends that never got the chance to live
the life I was blessed with on account of Vietnam.

(Their story in Chapter 7)

A Deer Gets Revenge

Stories from A Game Warden

by Sgt. John A. Walker

Sgt. Walker's first book

The U.P.
Upper Michigan

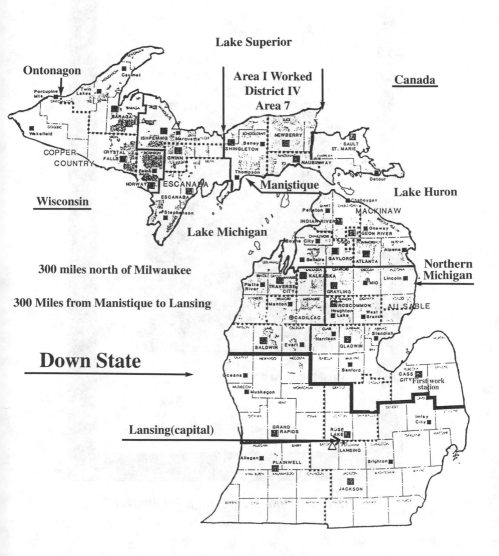

Lake Superior

Ontonagon

Area I Worked
District IV
Area 7

Canada

COPPER
COUNTRY

Manistique

Lake Huron

Wisconsin

Lake Michigan

Northern
Michigan

300 miles north of Milwaukee

300 Miles from Manistique to Lansing

Down State

First work
station

Lansing(capital)

A Bucket of Bones

Stories from
A Game Warden
by Sgt. John A. Walker

The second book by Sgt. John Walker

INDEX

Forwarned

This is the forth book in a series of humorous, backwoods, outdoor tales put together by retired Michigan Conservation Officer Sgt. John A. Walker. Just maybe this newspaper article, that sold hundreds and hundreds of his books, written by someone Sgt. Walker never met tells the story about his books best.

> "The language used ruined the whole book for me. I was not raised to talk that way, so I decided there must be a need for a book that people of all ages could read without having to hide from their kids or the kids hiding it from the parents."
>
> Sgt. John A. Walker retired
> game warden

Books Serve up Family-style Hunting Tales

By Mary Drier- Bay City Times-Tuscola County Advertiser

Hunting stories abound, but books by a former Tuscola County game warden offers a different point of view.

First, Sgt. John A. Walker is not only a hunter, but also a retired conservation officer. Second, he says his books are for the whole family and don't contain any of the bawdy tales sometimes associated with the sport.

Walker recently completed his third self-published book entitled "From the Land Where the 'Big' Fish Live".

"The books came about on the night I retired," said Walker. "Some friends that attended my retirement party gave me a great gift. It was a hard cover, leather bound book written by a game warden from another state."

"It seems like as if everybody likes a good game warden story, even a retired game warden."

While the gift was a nice idea, Walker objected to the strong language used in the book.

"Friends and family members asked if they could read the book when I was done with it, but I wasn't half way through the first chapter when I knew that I wouldn't let anyone read that book, " Walker said. "The language used ruined the whole book for me. I was not raised to talk that way, so I decided theremust be a need for a book that people of all ages could read without having to hide it from their kids or the kids hiding it from their parents." said Walker.

"From the hundreds of letters I've received, it appears there was a little niche for my style of book."

His first book was "A Deer Gets Revenge", and his second book was "A Bucket of Bones". All three books are humorous stories from the woods.

Walker has spent much of his life in the woods. He began his career in 1966 in Tuscola County when he took a job as a fire officer. He worked from the former Department of Natural Resources building on M-24.

In 1968, he became a game warden and stayed for eight years in Tuscola County before taking a promotion and transferring to Manistique in 1973.

From his job as a game warden, Walker wrote fishing reports for *The Manistique Pioneer Tribune.* Some of the reports on fishing included incidents from the game warden's life.

"The tales became more popular then the fishing reports," noted the author. "I never in my wildest dreams ever thought the books would go over like they have. Maybe I had a dream, but not enough faith."

Walker may have had little faith in his writing ability, but he does have plenty of faith. For more then 30 years, he worked as a game warden hunter safety instructor. For over 20 years, he worked with teenagers from the Bethel Baptist Church in Mansitique.

"I made a promise to the Lord and myself that if any of my books sold, I would place $1 from each book sold through me into a scholarship fund to help youth from the church I attend go off to college," said Walker.

As of August (96), his efforts have made it possible for 14 youth to receive $4,000.00 in scholarships.

"It is my dream that I will, with the Lord's help, be able to have enough in the scholarship fund so someday the interest can accumulate and make it possible to hand out scholarships for years to come, " stated Walker.

"The stories are from the heart of an old game warden that had the greatest job in the world. In doing this job, I heard many a great story and had more fun living some of them than any one person should be allowed, " said Walker.

Although most of the stories in the books relate to hunting and fishing, Walker notes a successful trip doesn't have to mean a trophy take.

"If we are going to continue to enjoy hunting and fishing, plus enjoy the great outdoors, we had better get back to the time when "success" does not decide whether we had a good time or not," said Walker.

"I may be in the minority of sportsmen, but I think we have lost the true love of hunting and fishing."

"I have written about it for years, and will keep on doing so till the day I ride off to that perfect deer blind in the sky. Never will getting or catching something decide whether or not I had a good time out in the woods."

"My dad taught me this point, I taught it to my kids and all my hunting buddies, and I will tell it to anyone who will listen. Enjoy being alive and healthy, enjoy just being out there and getting to be with the family and friends, enjoy the camp time, and if the good Lord should give you a "bonus" and you are successful, just add it to the great time you already had."

"Even if you do not hunt or fish, the outdoors is there for all of us to enjoy."

Besides being a successful writer, having sold over 20,000 books, he still writes his column for *The Manistique Pioneer Tribune.*

Cover

This is one of those pictures a young boy looks at all his life. It is my Dad's dad, Grandpa Walker.

I got this picture from hunting camp where it has been as long as I can remember. Dad always got a kick out of telling me the story about his dad's big deer. I guess this is one of the reasons a boy growing up in the backwoods grows up with his parents and grandparents as his heroes.

As I sit here and think back, I cannot really ever remember my Grandpa Walker ever being out of bed. You see, my Grandpa died of cancer back when I was a youth. Back in those days, they usually just sent you home. For a long time, my dad would drive his dad from Ontonagon to Ashland, WI, for treatments. As a youth I would get to ride along with them and listen to all their stories of years gone by.

Two things I really remember about these trips with grandpa. The first was that he owned one of those old Ford cars where they put the front doors on backwards. The other thing was, if Grandpa was feeling up to it, we would have to take a trip on the way back over to Matchwood and take the Norwich Road back home. It was on this road where the family homesteaded and Grandpa drove train in the woods. These were the bestest trips of all as Dad and Grandpa drove home this way and relived the "good old days".

On one of these trips, we ran into some ice on the roads. We came to a big hill on the Norwich Road called Deer Creek Hill. We made it down all right, but could not make it up the other side. As my Dad tried to get up the hill, he told me to put on Grandpa's old hunting coat, take his deer rifle, (empty, but it didn't matter) and go up on top of the hill and flag down any cars that came so they would not come over the hill and hit our car.

It may seem like a small thing to you, but not to a youth under ten, with a real hunting coat and a deer rifle, standing in the middle of the road, getting to be a man!

To this day, I cannot recall how Dad, with the help of those that stopped, ever got the old '32 Ford up the hill. I was just too busy being an important part of the whole deal to worry about the details.

The story of Grandpa's big deer and how he wished "He hadn't done that" is in this book.

Would you belive I got it!

Chapter-1
A True Yooper's Reality Check

I get asked all the time, "What's the U.P.? What's a Yooper and Yooper Land? Is it part of Michigan? "Well, that may really depend on who you are talking to or who you may ask.

It seems that no matter where you grow up at, that is the greatest place in the world to be a youth at. Back in the "good old days" of the 50's, there was just nothing like the U.P. Nothing like coming from good backwoods stock of a family that moved to the Ontonagon area to homestead and the other half coming out of Wisconsin to be part of the lumber era.

There were such great stories, and just to sit and listen to the "oldsters" talk about what they had been through could keep a boy dreaming forever.

My dad was always the type dad that would make a history lesson of the trips out hunting and fishing you took together. You soon made side trips to see an old trapper's cabin so far back in the woods you wondered how he ever got things back to it. Then there was the history behind Camp 2 and Camp 5.

When you went hunting it would be a trip something like this: You would take the main road up to the Correction Line, cut across through the woods to hit the old railroad grade called "The Main Line". You may go one way and hit the big potato fields (Where someone before you ever came along had tried to make their fame and fortune growing potatoes back in the middle of "No-where". The U.P. wilderness won out, and the potato farmer lost this one.) Or, you could go the other way to Camp 5 switch. These were the names and the directions that were given to a youth.

As you traveled with Dad, you learned the stories of yesteryear and what a time that must have been.

You soon learned that the people that made up the U.P. were a cross section of some very special people just like the cowboys that made the West famous in the Saturday afternoon movies.

I still sit and wonder on how these men back in the old days of the U.P. ever accomplished what they did. Dad told about taking large steam equipment up rivers, then across country through some woods and terrain that had to make these trips engineering marvels. He took you to old mine shafts, old logging camps, sites of towns and homesteads that were no longer there. Here he told you U.P. history and how "Yooper Land" came to be.

Now that you know how I learned to be, here are a few ways to see if you fit into the place of a True Yooper. (Someone who lives in Michigan's Upper Peninsula.)

Yooper Reality Check

It seems that there are so many people now-a-days that would like to be a "Yooper". I guess they just don't understand that to be a True Yooper there are some special characteristics that are required. Some people have them, some people never will.

With the fish not really hitting and hunting season over as far as I go, I have maybe too much time to sit around and think.

Are You A True Yooper?

Ifen, when you and the wifee are going out on a first class, dress up, social event, you put on your new white shirt and new tie, your three piece suit, vest and all, then you put your favorite hunters orange hat with a big buck on the front (a new one mind you), you just may be a True Yooper!

Ifen, when you just picked up the "new" pickup you just bought an it still has the dimmer switch on the floor, you just may be a True Yooper!

Ifen, when you are driving down the road in this "new" Yooper pickup you can keep track of the center line on the road by looking down at your feet, you just may be a True Yooper!

Ifen, when you pick up the weekly paper, the first things you check are the police reports, the court reports, and the death notices, you just may be a True Yooper!

Ifen, when you pick up the weekly paper you check the death reports first, you just may be a True Yooper over 50!

Ifen, you think a pair of dress shoes are felt-lined Sorel boots, you just may be a True Yooper!

Ifen, you buy your wife a pair of new felt-lined Sorel boots for Valentines Day, you are a True Yooper! In trouble!

Ifen, you are laying in the operating room at the local hospital about ready to be put under and you look up and the guy, with a big grin on his face, who is going to put you to sleep, you last saw at Thompson Creek after fish with a handnet, you may be a True Yooper!

Ifen, you think aerobic exercise is running a snow blower, you must be a True Yooper!

Ifen, you live in Michigan and are a true, die-hard, Green Bay Packer fan, you just must be a True Yooper!

Ifen, you think dress up, go to church clothes, are a Green Bay Packer hat and jacket, you just may be a True Yooper!

Ifen, when the kids are sick you give them Trenary Toast with warm milk and butter, you MUST be a True Yooper!

Ifen, you know the only good pasty comes with them there ruttabeggies in them, you just may be a True Yooper!

Ifen, your wifee is considered a single parent from September 15th through the end of December, you must be a True Yooper!

Ifen, you know that November 15th is a National Holiday, you must be a True Yooper!

Ifen, when your kids go off to college, they are wearing an old Ollie's Red Owl jacket, you know they are True Yooper's!

Ifen, when your kids go off to college they still cannot spell Tahquamenon, Ontonagon, Toivola, and Kinnickinnic, they must surely come from good True Yooper stock!

Ifen, after you graduate from college you still cannot spell, Tahquamenon, Ontonagon, Toivola, and Kinnickinnic, then surely you are a True Yooper with a college edumacation.

Ifen, you kids grow up thinking that venison is one of the three major food groups, you just may be a True Yooper!

Ifen, when your kids leave the nest they find out that the rest of the world has not even caught up with a lot of the words and sayings used by Mom and Dad in Yooper Land, they must come from good Yooper stock!

Ifen, you place the old snow tires off your old pickup on the back of your wifee's front wheel drive car, you just may be a True Yooper!

Ifen, (and this one is important) you have at least three sheds or out-buildings behind the house "full" of all those items you just may need someday and don't want to get rid of, you just may be, in fact you are, a True Yooper.

Ifen, your whole lifestyle changed when they closed the local dumps, where you used to return home with more then you took, you just may be a True Yooper!

Ifen, your buddy, from the Copper Country, wants the pickup truck makers to place the dimmer switch back on the floor, because he keeps getting his foot tangled up in the steering wheel, he may be a True Yooper!

There are more, but these will be a good reality check for a True Yooper!

Yooper Reality Check Number II

Ifen, you send your wife flowers for Valentine's Day and include the bill in the card, you just may be a True Yooper!

Ifen, you get all nervous and start to sweat when you see a stop light at an intersection, you just may be a True Yooper!

Ifen, you have to ask what a pasty is, you are NOT a True Yooper!!

Ifen, you have to ask if a pasty should have da rutabeggy in it, you are sure not a True Yooper!!

Ifen, your wifee uses the smoke alarm for her cooking instead of the ringing on the clock on the stove, you just must be a True Yooper!

Ifen, you agree with this saying, "It's raining in Gaylord, snowing in Marquette, and all the flakes are in Lansing", you just must be a Yooper.

Ifen, after fifteen years of successful hunting you have enough points to qualify for "Da Thirty Point Buck" patch you must be a Yooper.

Ifen, when you drive your "new to me" truck down the road, three out of four of your tires advertise for different companies, you could be a True Yooper!

Ifen, you put on your long handles in August and remove them the following May, while still taking a chance, you could be a True Yooper!

Ifen, you think picking up dime cans qualifies you for the Olympics you may be a True Yooper!

Ifen, your highest source of income is from picking up dime cans and picken greens, you just may be a True Yooper!

Ifen, when someone gives you directions in their town they say, "Go to the only stop light in town and take a left", you are in one of the main towns in Yooper land.

Ifen, you think the first day of spring starts with the smelt runs, you must be a True Yooper.

Ifen, you think that the "Mighty Mac Bridge" was a serious cause of pollution to the U.P., you must be a True Yooper!

Ifen, you think that travel from November 15th thru the 30th in Yooper Land should be restricted to only those that have family members or relatives living in the U.P., you must be a True Yooper!

Ifen, you think the creeks with the spring fish runs are kind of like stopping at a self-serve gas station on the way home with supper, you could be a True Yooper!

Ifen, your dad still uses Old Spice products and thinks they are the latest fad, you must be a Yooper's kid.

Ifen, you never had a sauna and are sitting there wondering what it is, you are sure not a True Yooper!

Ifen, you had never tried to kill your best buddy, back in your teenage years, by dumping ice water on the sauna stove, you cannot be a true Yooper!

After all this you will have the wisdom of a True Yooper youth and be able to write words of wisdom like this.

Ifen, you think a confederate-rebel is someone who wears a Detroit Lion's jacket, you must be a True Yooper with lots of wisdom.

Ifen, you think that the Green Bay Packers are paying half of the Detroit Lions coach's salary to keep him there, you must be a True Yooper.

Ifen, you think that biting off the head of a live smelt is the true test of manhood, you must be a True Yooper with a problem.

Ifen, you can talk your girlfriend into biting off the head of a live smelt, she is a True Yooper and both have problems.

Ifen, you are a Yooper Snowbird that goes south to Florida for the winter, then heads back home to Yooper land before May (The end of it!), you are a True Yooper that is dreaming!

Yooper Seasons

Now when a little Yooper boy
Begins to go to school,
He has to learn a lot of stuff
To prove that he's no fool.

He thinks his teacher's awful smart
To teach him math and readin',
Until that teacher tells him
  "Bout somethin called "four seasons".

Every true little Yooper boy
Knows what the seasons are.
He's known them ever since
He had a pacifier!

Every little Yooper knows
The first season is for birds.
Then deer season follows close
Before they all join in herds.

Next comes the hunt for rabbits
When the weather is a freezin!
And last of all in the spring
Comes the fishin' season.

Winter, spring, summer, fall,
These, the student reasons,
May be seasons in a book,
But they're not a Yooper's seasons!
                    Steve Seid

Me with dad's buck

Chapter-2
Hunting Shacks

I guess if you grew up back in the "good old days" in the backwoods there was just nothing like getting to spend time with the men from your family at hunting camp. The stories, the fact you were someone special, and learning from them, could life get any better?

In my books and my travels I have always said that some of the best times were not the actual hunt themselves, but the times spent together at camp.

In this chapter are the very vivid memories of my trips to camp as a youth; it seems like it was only yesterday. Plus, there are some tales sent to me by people that after hearing me talk know where my heart is.

A Paper Hunting Camp

Some things money cannot buy. One is the love a boy in the backwoods can have for his dad. How does a dad go about earning this love and respect from his boy? One of the best ways I have ever found is to make him your hunting buddy.

Back in the "good old days" before four wheel drives, orv's, and all the toys we have now, life was a lot more interesting.

Our hunting camp was way back in the woods off any main road. In fact, for a small boy under ten with short little legs, it was a whole lot farther back to camp then it would be now. If the fall conditions were right, we would use our old Ford "bug" to try and get back to camp. It was never any easy project.

Off we would go from the farm where our "bug" was kept, across the field, through the woods to the "Main Line". This was the old railroad grade where Dad and Grandpa used to run train. You would travel up the grade to the old fallen down shack called Camp #3.

Here we turned off the Grade to travel through the woods the rest of the way to hunting camp. Along the course of this road were mud holes, of Ontonagon red clay, where if you ever got stuck, and you usually did a time or two, you were really stuck.

If the fall was so bad that we could not get back to camp with the "bug", we would use a team of horses and a "jumper". Now, a jumper was a couple of logs with one end trimmed up in a curve. Between these logs were nailed some planks to stand on and place your supplies on. There was a cable or chain run through holes drilled in the front of the logs running up to the whipple-tree to hook the "jumper" up to the horses. I will say one thing, we never did get stuck on any of our trips with the horses.

When we finally made it to the area of our hunting camp on Mill Creek, I would have to say it was the one and only hunting camp of its kind I have ever observed in all my travels. This hunting camp had 2x2 studs in the walls covered by the heavy construction paper made at the paper mill in Ontonagon at the time. The roof was covered with tar paper. The camp was L shaped. In one part of the shack was an old wood cook stove. In the other part of the L was an old double bunk bed from an old logging camp. (This bed is in the hunting camp my brothers use to this day.) Against one wall was a spot for a little wood stove for heat.

One of our biggest problems each fall was to repair the holes in the walls made by animals. Porcupine were one of the main problems. For some reason they like to make a feast of any and all parts of the shack they could reach. Plus, along with the mice, they left a whole lot of left-overs that had to be cleaned out each year. BUT! These two critters were not our biggest problem!

It seemed that bear also liked our camp. Seeing the walls were made out of paper, the bear could walk into camp any place they liked right through the walls, look around and see what they could find, and then leave. The only thing was, they never seemed to leave camp through the same place in the wall they entered in through. It was interesting for a youth to check out all the claw marks in the wall's paper and try to fig-ure out how big the bear was that had visited during the past summer.

The trips in to fix up the camp were great, but the best part was when dad picked you up Friday during hunting season to take you out to camp for the weekend. You were ready whenever the chance came. In your red-plaid hunting outfit along with your trusty Red Ryder BB gun, you could handle any type critter a ten year old may run into! At least as long as dad was along.

You usually walked back into camp during hunting season doing a little hunting on the way. In fact, my best dad-son story is about one of these trips back in. It had turned really warm during hunting season this year. As we walked through the woods, Dad was on one side of the creek, and I walked along the other side. All of a sudden I heard my dad whistle, and this meant he had seen something, and I was to cross the creek to him.

I got to Dad's side of the creek, and he showed me a brush pile. As we looked at it, he explained that it was a bear's den. It seemed from the leaves clawed all around that the bear had moved out during the warm weather. Being the great outdoors man I was, I told Dad, "Maybe he's still in there?" My dad got down on his hands and knees to look into the den as I climbed up on top. As my dad was looking into the dark of the den trying to see if anything was in it, I (while standing up on top of the brush pile den) jumped up and down real hard to try and scare anything that may be in the den out.

As I came down from my super ten year old jump and hit the brush, I did not stop, but kept right on going through the brush into the bear den! As I entered the den from the top with a crash, the bear that was in the den decided it was time to leave the den as fast as he could! That is regardless of the fact my Dad was down on his hands and knees looking in through the den's opening! All of a sudden my dad and the bear were trying to occupy the same place at the same time, or should I say that my dad was now in fast reverse and the bear in fast forward!

Over backwards went my dad! By went the bear! And after the shock wore off, we laughed so hard we about died from laughter wondering what the bear thought.

Across the creek and on into hunting camp. Now, you have to remember there was no TV, no electricity, no nothing, but what was needed. The frig was a wooden box nailed to a tree with a door put on it. What a life! A young lad ate like a king at hunting camp and was treated like one of the guys.

Every night at 6:00 sharp we turned on the radio that was Grandpa
Walker's to listen to the "Deer Hunters' Round-up" out of Ironwood.
This radio was something special. It was huge, by today's standards,
and took a battery that was made up of at least a zillion flashlight batteries all wired together. The battery alone weighed at least a ton to a
young lad. The key to using this radio was to make sure you just turned
it on for the news in the morning and the round-up at night. If you did
this the battery would last for most of deer season. I still have this old
radio and one of the batteries.

Usually at night the men would play a couple of hands of cribbage. This
is why I thought the right way for a boy to count was 15-2, 15-4, and a
pair is 6.

After this it was into bed, and what a bed it was! No matter how many
people were in camp, and there were usually four men, there were still
only the two double bunk beds. These beds had on them what you
called a straw tick. These were flour sacks all sewed together making up
a big bag. Into this bag you stuffed straw to fill it up and this was
placed on the bed. I'll tell you right now, you've never had a good
night's sleep till you've slept in a straw tick between Dad and Uncle
Randall. In fact, a youth of ten was in danger of sinking out of sight in
the bed.

In the morning the cook got up, lit a fire, and crawled back into bed till
it got going and warmed things up. Then breakfast was cooked, and we
all got up to eat. After everything was cleaned up, it was time to make
plans for the day and head off hunting with Dad.

I guess the worst time of the year for a young boy like myself was the
time when it was the end of another deer season. Camp gear would be
stored away into the big wooden boxes, everything would be cleaned
up, the hunting log written on the wall of camp by the door would be
brought up to date, then it was off to return to civilization.

The only thing I can recall being good about this day was that using the
bathroom was going to be a little warmer and a little more comfortable.

Since I have been writing these outdoor tales, I have received dozens of
stories from all over the state. This is one of those sent to me about a
deer camp I spent many a night at with my dad.

But Honey, You'll Love It

Maybe a better title would be "How to start a marriage off right".

It seems that this couple, from down in the "Thumb" area of lower Michigan, got married and came up to "Yooper Land" for their "Honey's"-moon. They had made plans to spend their special time together on Mackinac Island. Could there be a better place for a young couple to start their life out together? Newlyweds, trapped on an island!

But after a while new-hubby got to thinking, and this could prove to be dangerous. "Seeing we're already up here in the U.P., why don't we take a trip over to deer camp so I can show it to you?" O'why not, after all it is his honey-moon time too, and if it will keep him happy, she thought. (Mistake number one)

Off the two newlyweds go on this little side trip to "his" deer camp. The side trip lead from the beauty and security of Mackinac Island, to the black flies and mosquitoes of the deep, black woods off the Norwich Road all the way over in Ontonagon County! But, after all this was special to "him".

Now please understand, back in those days when you went into deer camp, as the first story tells, it was a project. Usually to get into a camp like this, these men hired a local farmer (my uncle) with his team of horses. This deer camp was an old logging camp that had been sold to these men when all the timber had been cut off. To get into them there were roads, in spots, between the red clay mud holes and beaver ponds. So, once in a great while as you hike back into camp you did have a good walking area. But for the rest of the time, old well.....

So here are our newlyweds, the guy in his glory going back in to show his new bride his pride and joy, deer camp, and the wifee now wondering if step one should have ever taken place back down in the Thumb area. Our new bride had packed for her dream honey-moon to be spent in civilization back on Mackinac Island or somewhere like it. Not for a back packing trip through the woods to deer camp, **but!** The best is yet to come.

Off they go, as she told me, "With weeds that grew over my head, the walks across beaver dams, then through or around mud holes, till after a number of miles we did hit easier walking the last number of miles into camp. **but!** it was his honeymoon too, so....."

After they got to camp, and with the pride that only a true owner of a Yooper deer camp could have, he showed his new bride around. (In fact, as far as deer camps go, this camp is triple AAA rated and really, really nice, almost.) **but then!!!** Surprise number two!!

As our newlywed hubby informs his newlywed wifee, "It is too late to make our long trip back out today. It would be dark before we ever got back to the main road and the car. So, we might as well spend the night here at deer camp and head out in the morning". Tricky!!

As this lady put it in her letter to me, "With all that mice and porcupine **"feces"** laying all over the place!" (Now, you know for sure she was not a "True Yooper" because most Yoopers don't call it that.)

But, the honeymoon must have worked for this story was written and sent to me after many-many years together. Although she never did say if she ever went back into hunting camp again.

Lucky Laces

One Sunday morning, right after deer season, I was standing in the back of church and this lady came up to me and said, "John, we had the best deer season we ever had this year! It was just like your stories where what takes place is more important then what you get. Our grandson was at camp for the first time, and what a time we had!"

This is her story as she told it to me.

It all started out the night before season at a camp up north of Manistique. (This crew spends a lot of time up in Yooper Land during the hunting seasons and are from the area where I used to work down state.)

On this evening, the boss of the camp, or so he thought, put his foot down. It seems that his wife, the grandma telling me this story, had a pair of hunting boots she had worn for years. The laces in grandma's boots were so old and dry rotted and had been tied together so many times, that the boss gave her some new ones and told her to get rid of the old laces!!

Grandma protested this move because these were her lucky deer hunting laces. We all know where grandma is coming from because all "good" hunters have their little tricks to improve their odds when it comes to getting a deer. But, the boss is the boss, so Grandma changed her lucky laces for the new ones. But there is more then one way to win out in the end as we will find out.

The next day deer season opens and wouldn't you know it, it wasn't long till Grandma had the biggest buck in camp! New laces and all. But when the truth of the story came out, Grandma had to reach into her hunting coat pocket and pull out the pair of old, worn out, boot laces! Grandma's lucky laces had produced once more, even if they were no longer in her boots.

After a couple of days of fruitless hunting, the grandson came up to Grandma and asked, "Grandma, how about lending me your lucky laces to use today?" What could a grandma say! So, off went the grandson on a hunt with Grandma's lucky laces now in his coat pocket.

Would you believe that by the time the crew got back into camp that night Grandma no longer had the biggest buck on the buck pole for this year. Guess who had it? You are right. Grandma's lucky laces had produced once more.

As Grandma told me, "You could not have purchased the feelings and the time had at deer camp that night for a million dollars. Money could never buy the time we had this year."

And standing there listening and watching her as she told me the story, you could tell she was telling the story from her heart.

She also told me that on the last night at camp the crew held an auction and Grandma's "Lucky Laces" were sold to the highest bidder.

I have to wonder what next year will bring, if nothing else, a ton of memories as stories are told and retold.

Off on a hunt

Chapter-3
Game Warden's Wifee

For some reason after writing the tales in the books like I do, I received a number of calls asking about the life of being a Game Warden's wife.

I really think there are a lot of changes from what my wife had to do and the modern day better half. Here are a few things that took place with the wifee being along and part of it.

First: **He's A Conservation Officer**

The training is over and the uniform is in hand,
You immediately see how tall he now stands.

With ideas and plans to make everything right,
No violating, no gun shots, no trouble, no fights.

The wives must sit and wait and listen,
While the husbands attack their vital mission.

To do their job the best that they can,
To work to protect things for their fellow man.

He comes home late and sometimes grumpy,
His supper re-heated and sometimes lumpy.

He works, then sleeps, then works again,
His wife says "Good-bye" and is alone again.

She copes with the kids and launders the clothes,
But when husband calls she immediately goes.

To soothe his wounds and cure his ills,
And try not to mention the monetary bills.

The calls in the nights, the worry, the scare,
And many a night a silent little prayer.

She hopes that he is happy and strong and alert,
Because if he is not he is bound to get hurt.

He may fight violators in the woods, drunks in a park,
But his wife is still waiting at home all alone.

She waits for the hour, the familiar face,
He's home once again from the eternal rat race.

Five days of work and now two days off,
But not enough time for one round of golf.

Johnny needs shoes and Cathy a dress,
Not even enough time for peace and some rest.

But he continues on through good times and strife,
Because at his side stands a Game Warden's wife.

There is no way in the olden days that a Game Warden could ever do the job he did without the help of a wife willing to be at his side. For 25 years I had one of the best partners any Game Warden could have. Maybe this little poem somebody wrote tells it best between the lines what the wives put up with.

A True Watch Dog

More then once during my working time, we would get up in the morning and see foot prints in the snow where somebody had been around the house. One time after catching some violators with a deer, they broke into the field office buildings trying to get the evidence back. When they couldn't find it there, they came and looked around the house for it.

On this evening my wife and I had both been asleep in bed for quite a while. All of a sudden, the German Shepherd dog I had let loose!!

If you have ever had a good dog, you can usually tell if he is barking at an animal or something else. On this night the way he was barking, I knew right away someone was out in the yard.

I got out of bed, pulled on my pants, (thank Goodness) and headed downstairs. As I went to the back door, all this being done without turning any lights on in the house, I went by the frig. Up on top of the frig was an old army 30 caliber carbine, with a banana clip. I grabbed this and quietly went out the back door. Moved along the side of the house to the front corner.

About this time I could see some bodies through the trees coming from the area towards the river that ran behind the house. As they got closer, I could hear them singing!

When they walked into the drive, there I stood with a rifle, as a pastor, his daughter, and another couple from town appeared. It seems that they were canoeing on the river and got lost. It was well after mid-night when they got back near town, and I lived in the closest house.

The word must have got around, about me and my rifle, because this was the last time anyone ever came poking around my house in the dark.

Phone Calls and Visitors

Back in the "Good Old Days", the local game warden worked right out of his house. This meant that he sold beaver licenses from his home, received 95% of all phone calls at his home, and even had those he spent a lot of time looking for coming to his home. When Hubby was out working, guess who was the one at home that had to handle all these things? You guessed right! Wifee.

During this evening, as we sat at supper, I received a couple of those phone calls that all officers who work in a small area, where everybody knows them, seem to receive. This caller, who I knew, but he would not say who he was. He just wanted to express his opinion about myself and some things he would like to see happen to me.

An officer gets used to these things, but there is no way you can ever get a wife used to having this happen.

(The one thing I did do was to get a referee's whistle, a good loud one, and place it by the phone. The rule for my wife and kids was, if someone did not want to tell you who they were and just wanted to rip you up with foul language, take the whistle and blow it as hard as you can into the phone! This really cut down on the number of crank calls coming into the house.)

As dark rolled around, on this evening, my partner picked me up and we went out to work shiners. We covered a lot of ground and had a pretty good night.

While going towards Inland Quarry on the Green School Road, we were traveling without headlights, and we saw a car shining. There was not any place to pull off the road, so we pulled over to the right hand side as far as we could and waited on the car.

After a little while it was as close as it could get before their headlights would light up the patrol car, so we pulled on our headlights, hit them with both spotlights, and floored the patrol car to get to them as quick as we could.

As we cut in front of them to stop them, a party jumped out of the passenger side of the car that had been shining and took off running. The school teacher was out of the patrol car almost as quick and hot in his footsteps. I jumped out and shined my flashlight into the area where they had run off the road.

Here I saw two men standing in waist deep water! It seems it was just a little wet here in the woods where our violator decided to run. As I shined my flashlight on him, he hauled back and threw the firearm he had as far out into the water as he could. This did not make the game warden too happy.

As the teacher, who was working with me, and the violator came out of the water onto the road, I went up to him. I told him, "You have two choices. Number 1, you can wade out into the water and bring the rifle back out to me. Or, Number 2, I will have to go into the water and get it, and if I do, you will never see that rifle again!" He told me he was not about to go get it.

I did not look forward to wading around in water up to my waist, in the woods, in the dark. I collected the evidence from the two that had been shining and went back to my patrol car. Here I radioed to the State Police Post and asked them to do me a favor. "Go by my house, wake up my wife, and tell her I need to have my waders that are hanging out in the out-building behind the house." The Troops went by the house, and the wifee had to get out of bed and go back to the building so the Troops could bring my waders to me.

When the Troopers got to the area where I was waiting, I pulled on my waders and went gun-hunting back in the water. After looking for a minute, I found a brand new 300 Savage rifle with a scope.

Being true to my word, when we went to court I filed papers to have the party's rifle, spotlight, and hunting knife forfeited to the state. But, things got worse for our night hunter.

It seems that the day, of the night I caught him, he had gone down to one of the local hardware stores and bought this new 300 Savage Rifle with a scope. He had signed a loan with the store to make payments on the firearm and had placed one payment down. The judge ordered him to forfeit his new rifle, spotlight, and knife, AND he was ordered to keep making the payments on his now gone rifle till it was paid off!! **(Rabbit Trail:** The next night while working off River Road east of town, we were again running without lights. A pickup truck pulled onto the road in front of us and went slowly down the road. We were right behind it. It came to an area of an orchard and stopped. We could see the passenger moving around in the truck, and then something was thrown out the window. We waited a minute till they started using a spotlight and stopped them. As we pulled up, we saw a new box that a spotlight came in laying in the road. As we approached the pickup, we saw why they had to buy a new spotlight!! It was our two guys from the night before!! Some people never learn.)

Back To Wifee.....

After I got home from working, the night my wife had to get up and go get my waders, I found out she had not been sleeping too well anyway. It seems that this party that had made the phone calls at supper time the night before was not satisfied with just doing this. Seeing I was not at home, he thought it would be cute to go by the house and shine it with a spotlight and see if he could upset the family.

The next morning when I was at the State Police Post, I was telling the Troops what had happened to my wife and family while I was out on patrol. One of the Troops, a big Swede, said, "Come on, let's go for a ride."

We got into the State Police car, and he drove right over to the party's house that had been calling and now was monkeying around my house. He walked up to the front door, and when the caller-shiner came to the door, told him to get into the patrol car as he wanted to talk with him.

As we sat there, I never said a word, but this big Trooper turned around, looked the party right in the eyes and said calling him by name, "Let me tell you something. You feel like calling us officers names, all right we are used to it. If you feel like playing games with us, OK, it's part of the job. If you want to give us a hard time, go for it, we can live with it. BUT, if I ever hear of you giving this officer's wife or family, or any other officer's family, a hard time again you will personally answer to me! AND, if I'm not enough, I guarantee you will answer to everyone wearing a badge. Pick on us, that's part of the job. Pick on our families, you have crossed over the line!! Do you understand what I'm telling you?"

The party said only one word, "Yes."

The Trooper got out of the car, let the party out, and we drove back to the post. There is no way I could ever thank him for what he did. That put an end, in our small town, to anymore activity involving my home and family.

A Romantic Drive

One time there was a real problem with all the ORV's tearing up the sand dunes along Lake Michigan. There was no way you could catch them using a marked patrol unit. If you got close, and they saw you, off they went.

So, the boss told me to use my old pickup on patrol and see if I could catch some of the 4-wheelers.

One evening I asked the wifee if she would like to go for a ride. It was a beautiful summer evening. Why not take your favorite girl for a moon-light ride down along the Lake Michigan beach?

We left town and went down to the shore along the gravel road that follows the beach. We had been driving for a little while, enjoying the beauty of nature, the time together, and just relaxing. As we came into an area where there used to be a park, I saw a couple of 4-wheelers tearing across the sand dunes. Off we went!!

I tried to get down this gravel road, down a two track, onto the beach before they got there to see if I could catch them. (My wife soon knew there was an ulterior motive for our little moonlight romantic ride.)

My pickup only had one little problem! It seemed in the sand and gravel as you were flying along down the road, when you hit the brakes, the right side, front brake would lock up, and you would make a hard right hand turn whether you wanted to or not. We made a few of these, and I could tell without even looking that my wifee was really enjoying the ride.

I finally made it to the two track and caught one of the ORV's. Out from under the seat I pulled my ticket book and issued him a ticket. (After all, I couldn't have my ticket book on the seat or else wifee might have figured things out.)

After giving this party a ticket, we headed back towards the park. I figured my wifee must really be enjoying the evening out with me because she was not saying a word, just looking out at the pretty trees on her side of the road.

As she was enjoying this, all of a sudden the other 4-wheeler came flying out of the woods right in front of us, and off we went chasing it! Back to the park, down the park trail, off he went across the dunes, and we had to stop. (The front hard-right brake was still working fine.)

I got out of the pickup and walked back into the dunes the way the ORV had run. Would you believe it! About two dunes back here I found the ORV where the driver had jumped off and run back into the woods. I went back to the pickup, dropped the tail gate, and backed up to the sand dune.

Wifee asked me what I was doing? I told her I had found the 4-wheeler and was going to load it up and take it with us. I could tell right away that everything else that had taken place on our moonlight ride was minor compared to the thrill she got when I told her this. In fact, if I recall right, she rather loudly said," **YOU can't DO THAT !!!!!!!!**"

I loaded up the 4-wheeler, and we left the area to head back for town. As we passed River Road, I saw this pickup parked at the stop sign. I thought nothing of it and kept on for town. When there, I pulled into the State Police Post to tell them if they should have someone come in looking for an ORV to tell them I have it.

As I pulled into the parking lot, the pickup that had been stopped at the stop sign pulled in behind me. As I got out of my pickup this guy walked up and said, "What are you doing with my 4-wheeler?" If I recall right in the dark, it was night time now, my wife was trying to hide in the glove box.

The party told me his teenage boy had left the house with the ORV, and he had just started out looking for him. Well, we worked things out, so wifee could get home, because I was sure by this time she was tired of being a junior game warden.

Illegal Buck that was shot at night and left.

Chapter-4
Buddies in Uniform

There is nothing like working with a crew of young men in law enforcement. When working in this field all hours of the days and nights you get to really be good friends. One of the things you soon learn is the personalities of each officer and who to watch out for before you get taken by one of them.

Here are a couple of stories that still bring a laugh to me as I write them.

But, She Should Have Known Better

There is one thing you soon learn working law enforcement that you had better watch out for.

It is perfectly all right to pass a cruddy job, down to some other agency, or another officer who is dumb enough to accept it. When this happens it seems at times the bottom of the list is where the Lowly Conservation Officer is at. The only one below him to pass it on to is the janitor, and he doesn't get out on the road too often.

On this particular day I was out on patrol enjoying a nice warm sunny spring day. I could justify almost anything I wanted to do during this time of year so had not a care in the world. That is until the dispatcher from the local sheriff office got hold of me on the radio.

She informed me that they had a report of a dead horse laying in a ditch and would I go check it out. **GIVE ME A BREAK!!** What in the world did a game warden have to do with horses living or dead! But it seems that the sheriff department's rational was, spring, dead horse in ditch, spring means water may run through ditch finding dead horse in it's path, water becomes polluted, polluted water's DNR problem, therefore dead horse now belongs to local game warden!!

I took a ride out where the dead horse was supposed to be, and sure enough, there it was. As I arrived, a sheriff department car arrived also.

We put our heads together trying to figure out what in the world do you do with a dead horse! Then we figured it out.

On the radio, I contacted the same dispatcher at the sheriff department and asked her, "Can you look up on the shelf where all the Secretary of State books are and find the brand book and see who owns the double O brand?"

Our problems were over seeing there was no water near the dead horse and it was out in the middle of no-where, so off we went.

A couple of days later I stopped by the sheriff's department for coffee. As I went into the coffee room, the dispatcher came in and told me, "I have looked all over the office, in every book I could find, without any luck in locating that Secretary of State brand book. I would hate to say how many hours I have spent looking for it." As everybody in the coffee room just broke out laughing!!

I all of a sudden did not feel like having a cup of coffee, seeing this dispatcher was a red head, with a little fire in her system. I thought it may be wise for this old game warden to head out the nearest door as she was about to find out there is no such thing as a Secretary of State brand book!! She had spent all this time looking for something that never was.

But! Officer

In years gone by when all the youth seemed to have one of these fast cars like a GTO, 442, Chevy SS, it was nothing to try to stop a car and get into a high speed chase. Believe it or not, most officers when they became wise enough to understand what the results of these chases could be, did not like them.

On this night patrol I was working by myself looking for deer shiners in the state game area. All of a sudden I received a call from the sheriff department that one of their cars was chasing a car. This fleeing car was coming from the south into the area where I was working.

As they came through the main intersection still going north, I was off to the west of them. All of a sudden I heard the deputy say, "He just turned off the highway going west on Wells Road!"

A really bad move for a party trying to escape!

You see Wells Road we always heard was an old stagecoach road. If true, from those days with the stagecoach using the road, it had never been improved. In places this road was still a corduroy road. (This means that years ago when a road went through a real wet, muddy area, the people using it would cut trees and lay them crossways on the road so you could drive on them.) Needless to say this area was rough. But, you see this section of the old road was the good section of it. In other places there were mud holes where the stagecoach could get stuck, and you would have to stand on the roof to get out.

As the deputy followed the car he was trying to stop down Wells Road, another police car approached it from the other end. Once you were on this road, you had only two ways to go, forward or back the way you came from.

As I approached the area, I heard radio traffic that went something like this. Deputy chasing, "Can you see the car?" Police car on the other end, "NO, but I can see headlights coming at me." A few minutes later, "The headlights are still coming my way. NO! The headlights just went out of sight!!"

As all the law enforcement cars approached the area where the head-lights were last seen, we found the fleer's car. He had also found one of those mud holes big enough to hide a stagecoach. Here he sat looking at a car sitting with water filling up the inside and now running over the hood.

The deputy that had first tried to stop him got some ID and took the driver back to his patrol unit. After things were checked out and tickets were issued, all the law enforcement officers were standing there thinking about the poetic justice that had just taken place. The deputy and the driver returned to the car in the mud hole.

As most of the officers got ready to leave and were walking back to their patrol cars, the driver of the car still sitting in the middle of the mud hole came up to the deputy. Our driver had obviously not learned a thing, for looking at the deputy he ordered, did not ask, "Call me a wrecker!!" (You could add a few more choice words about what he thought of law enforcement officers to this order.)

The deputy without cracking a smile walked up to him and patting him on the back said as serious as could be, "OK buddy, you're a wrecker!" As we all got in our cars and left with him still standing there with a dumb look on his face, thinking, "That is not really what I had in mind."

Friends?

On this evening, during goose season, I was working in the Cooks area with another officer.

We had hidden our patrol unit behind an old shack along side an orchard so we could cross the road and sneak into a field to wait for late shooters. (There are set times that you have to stop hunting waterfowl. It is usually about ten minutes before all the ducks and geese arrive to the area you are hunting.)

This evening we had a little luck, and after running through the orchard across the road into the field, we caught two people shooting at geese after dark.

After tickets were issued to the two, we headed back toward the place where we had parked the patrol car. As we were walking along talking, the officer working with me all of a sudden realized that he had lost his pistol out of his holster in our travels.

We hunted all over on the field side of the road for it with no luck. We then made our way back to the area of the orchard and were looking for the pistol in the long grass under the old apple trees. As we were look-ing, we heard a vehicle coming down the road from the north, so we shut off our flashlights and waited for the vehicle to go by.

Right when this vehicle was in front of us, (not knowing it) it slammed on it's brakes, turned crossways in the road with it's headlights covering part of the orchard and the old shack. A spotlight came on, and we heard two quick shots!!

I say we heard two quick shots! Because about this time we were both trying to crawl into a non-existant hole in the ground out in the middle of the orchard!!

As the vehicle backed up to leave, we raised our heads up and saw a law enforcement emblem on the door. We knew there was no way they were violating after all the talking and running around we had just been doing in the orchard. BUT, we figured seeing they had scared the fire out of us why not return the favor!

When we got back into town, we went to their office. The sergeant sitting at the desk was one of those I knew would go along with us. So he got out one of their official complaint pads and wrote the following on it: Time: place: then, a patrol car with all the markings on it came from the north down such and such a road, all of a sudden stopped in the area of an orchard, a spotlight was cast into the area of the orchard and two shots were fired. The police car then left at a high rate of speed.

A couple hours later when the two officers returned from their patrol and walked into the office, the sergeant just tossed the complaint pad up on the desk and said, (without cracking a smile) "You two had better read that!"

He told me later he thought the one party was going to pass out, as they saw their whole career pass before their eyes! All the other one could say over and over was, "It was a cat, only a cat!"

We did return the next day and found the officer's pistol.

An illegal treehouse for hunting.

Chapter-5
Yesteryear

I don't care where you worked or what you did in life, the changes since the end of the BIG war have been almost unreal.

I can remember going out to the Ontonagon airport to watch the planes, any plane was something to see. The ones we watched were bi-winged and Piper Cubs, and we really thought they were something.

I can remember when your Federal Income Tax form was just a post-card! **Really!** All you did was fill out a postcard, sign it, and mail it in!

I can remember when times got bad the local, corner store must have carried most of the people in town from payday to payday. Sometimes I think they had more money outstanding than the banks did up town. It makes you wonder how they did it and what would life have been like if they had not.

I can remember being able to get a whole pile of candy for five cents. Getting into the movie for kids on Saturday for nine cents, so you would have a penny left for the candy counter.

I can remember the first time I saw a pop machine, a bottle for a nickel, I drank so much I about got sick.

I can remember when 90% of the houses in town took the same key for the doors. If you went on vacation, if you did not have a key, you borrowed the neighbors to lock your doors. This was the only time they were ever locked, when you were going to be gone for a week or two.

I can remember when hunting camps were never locked. Most had just a wooden peg holding the door shut. If you were on a back-pack hunting trip you were welcome to use the camp. Just sign the note book telling who you were and when you used it, replace any wood you may have used, and leave it like you found it.

I can remember when there were no speed limits after you left the city limits. In fact the sign read, **end of speed zone!**

I can remember when you took a ride with mon and dad that you came to the end of the power lines. Then dad would say, "The houses from here on do not have any electric lights, they still have to use lanterns." I thought this was really great, but remember it wasn't usens that was doing it.

I can remember when dad would not believe that car tires could ever hold air without an inner-tube in them. In fact for years dad would still have the garage put a tube in all the tires he bought just to be safe. You just cannot trust some of these new ideas.

I can remember owning snowmobiles and ORV's before there were any laws telling you who, how, when, and where.

I can remember when you treated your school teachers with respect! If you did do something wrong, you hoped and prayed that Dad never found out about it.

I remember when, if you got corrected at school it was not the teacher's fault.

I can remember when you had better bring home a good report card, and not brag about the slips you got for misbehaving.

I can remember when coffee went from a nickel to a dime! Dad thought the world was going off the deep end. (I paid $1.00 for a cup last week)

After Getting Married:

I can remember getting five loaves of bread for $1.00.

I can remember getting five dozen eggs for $1.00.

I can remember when **all canned** goods, except a can of milk, were ten cents a can, and chickens were twelve to fifteen cents a pound.

I can remember when you could not put $5.00 worth of gas into your 27 gallon gas tank.

I can remember when you bought gas you could save green stamps to purchase things when Christmas shopping.

I can remember when you pulled into a gas station they filled your gas tank for you, checked your oil and radiator, took your money and brought back your change.

I can remember when you could fill your fuel oil tank for under $20.00.

I can remember buying a brand new car for $2,000.00. My dad would then pull out his slip where he bought a new one for $500.00.

I can remember when you could buy a pair of new snowmachines and a trailer for $600.00.

I can remember when your word was a contract, more binding than anything ever put on paper.

I can remember when bad debts were a disgrace, and you would die before you ever got one.

I can remember when working was a respected occupation.

I can remember when taking care of your wife and children was expected of a man and if you did not, you were worse than a bum.

I can remember when being loyal and honest was expected of all people, even politicians.

I can remember when those working a job paid for by the tax payers were called "public servants" and expected to listen to them and help them out, not force feed them with their opinions and ideas.

I can remember when a grandpa was the best story teller in the world, before TV came along and story telling became a lost art.

Being a Game Warden:

I can remember when you drove your own car for a patrol car.

I can remember when you got hand-me-down uniforms from the department tailor for the first fifteen years you were on the job.

I can remember when a uniform was a uniform, and if your boots had a white sole on them you died it black or paid the price.

I can remember when judges did not have to be lawyers.

I can remember when outlaws went to jail for their crimes if they didn't have money to pay their fines.

I can remember when a two cell flashlight was the best piece of electronic equipment you had.

I can remember the piece and quiet of the world before someone invented the computers and all the work they bring about.

I can remember when you spent 90% of your time catching bad guys instead of filling out forms and doing paper work.

I can remember when officer's personally bought almost all their own equipment or hoped the State Police would save their old flashlight batteries for them.

I can remember when the gas that went into your patrol car cost the state 9 cents a gallon.

I can remember when the hunters and fishermen were considered the friends of the outdoors, not the special interest groups.

I can remember when almost all the Conservation Officers you worked with were war vets.

I can remember when the older officers you work with told a story you had to try and figure out what decade they were talking about.

I can remember when marine safety belonged to the sheriff department, traffic and drunks to the State Police, and fish and game violations to the Conservation Officers.

I can remember when if a Conservation Officer used a snowmachine it was one he owned.

I can remember when in the fall of the year the Fire Officer and the Game Warden were a team and spent the whole fall working together.

I can remember when the Game Warden drove his car anyplace a 4-wheel drive pickup could go and some where a pickup couldn't go because it was all we had.

I can remember when the Game Warden kissed his wifee good-by the first of October because he would be working everyday till the end of deer season.

I can remember when an officer could tell the vehicles that were using spotlights by how yellow looking and dim their headlights would be.

I can remember when 21 shrimp in a basket, with fries, coffee, and a piece of pie was $.89.

Illegal Deer

Chapter-6

Proper Training
(But Maybe Not Too Bright)

I always get asked if there were any times when you were really scared or really in danger out there while working as a Game Warden.

When you talk about this you have to look at things two different ways. I will let you guess which is which.

First, there are the times when officers can run into something they have no control or choice over that puts them into bad situations. I guess all people that work in any type law enforcement work face these times.

Second, and maybe those most often, are the times when young officers, just maybe, engage their energy before they engage their brain. This sometimes can get you into a whole lot of scary situations.

Here are a number of short tales of what I mean.

Full Speed Ahead !!!

One of the first things you must understand, is the fact that back when I started as a Conservation Officer, you got 95% of your training "on the job". They would put you to work with some of the older officers in the area where you were going to be working to learn the job from them. Some of these officers were rather interesting to work with. In fact, you soon began to wonder if or how they ever lived through some of their patrols.

I have always said, that when a Game Warden gets to heaven, he will see a Guardian Angel or maybe more then one, with a blank look on his face, with a big nervous twitch, staring off at nothing, trying to figure out how he ever got this way. It is easy to figure out, he got this way from riding around with your average game warden.

Jim

The sergeant who I was first assigned to work with was an x-Detroit officer. I swear this guy could see in the pitch, black of the darkest night. This means that using headlights was something you only did while traveling on a main road, when you had to.

On this night, Jim picked me up at my house that was out in the State Game Area. As we were walking to the car, we observed a spotlight beam go across the sky a couple miles to the north of us. We jumped into Jim's patrol car, and off we went. As we came into the area where we figured the shiners had to be working, Jim killed his headlights.

This was one of those nights that it was darker than dark. No moonlight, nothing to help you out. We pulled into an intersection, and looking down the road to the west, we saw a vehicle. This vehicle was parked where we knew there were some fields. It was all state game area land from where we were to the highway about five miles away. The people in the vehicle were shining a spotlight out of the passenger side of the car.

Jim pulled onto the road the shiner's vehicle was parked on, floored the patrol car, and yelled, "Watch for the ditch on your side!!"

WATCH FOR THE DITCH!!! How could I watch for the ditch when I could not even see the dash of the car! Let alone the road which I assumed was under the car somewhere?!

All that Jim did was aim for the shiner's tail-lights and head for them. In this county where we were working, almost all the roads were straight as could be, so at least there were no curves.

After we covered the three miles to their car, doing at least 60-70 miles an hour without any headlights, (you have no idea how fast this seems to the passenger in the patrol car) we flew up behind their car and turned on our lights and jumped out to run up to their car.

In it we found two violators, with the spotlight, and a shotgun with buckshot. So if you have cat-eyes, as any good game warden must, it helps out.

If He Can ! I Can!

There was another time I was out on night patrol with a fire officer. We were working an area for shiners and had hidden down a two-track off a gravel road.

After we had been there for a while, this vehicle came down the road from our left and passed through the intersection going north. I pulled up into the intersection, without any headlights, to watch this vehicle. When it got down the road about a mile from where we sat, we all of a sudden saw a spotlight being used from the car.

Nothing to this, I had been trained by a pro, right? I turned towards the car that was shining, (the road was straight as could be), aimed for the tail lights, and half-floored the patrol car, (I was still on my learners permit.) Off we went, I knew this area well.

From having worked this area a number of times before, I knew there was one little, bitty problem between me and the shiners. It seems about two-thirds of the way towards them there was this bridge. But, this bridge was a little bit narrower than the road we were on. No problem, I paced myself to where I figured the bridge was, turned the car into the middle of the road a little to compensate for the bridge, and we continued across the bridge after the car we wanted to stop.

Suddenly the car shook, with a loud twang of metal bouncing off metal. I slammed on the brakes and turned on my headlights, shiner or no shiner!

Would you believe that the County Road Commission must have moved that silly bridge a couple hundred feet farther north since the last time I was through here! **but,** we only missed, missing it by a little.

Lucky? Or That Guardian Angel?

On this patrol I was working alone on a holiday, the 4th of July. Back during these days we never had radio contact with any other law enforcement agency. Plus, on a holiday, our office was usually closed.

As I started out, I was going to patrol some of the state game area that was closed to camping. I went down the main highway heading over to the game area. When going by a two-track, too wet and muddy to travel, I saw a car parked down it. I stopped, backed up, and went down to check it out.

Sitting in the middle of a mud hole was a newer, clean as a whistle Caddy. It did not fit as a car that someone running around the game area would use, to neat and clean looking. So I got out of my patrol unit and looked the area over. I could not find anyone and the car had been there for a little while.

I got back into my patrol unit and backed out to the highway to head off on my way. Nothing I could do if the people had already walked somewhere for help.

A little while later, when I was coming to a little town, I saw a city and sheriff department car parked at a coffee shop. I went in to join them, and while talking, I told them about the car I had just checked out in the game area that did not look right. I gave the deputy the license number off the Caddy. After coffee we went our different ways.

In the late afternoon, when heading back towards home, I passed a sheriff car. He turned around and flagged me down. We got out to talk, and he asked me if the car I had observed that morning was still there. I said I didn't know because I had went up north after the coffee stop.

He then told me that the car was stolen that morning and the two men in it had robbed and shot a gas station attendant.

Later, when they were caught, they told about getting stuck in the mud and walking up to an old barn farther down the road. Here they tore off some boards to place under the wheels to get their car out.

It must have been while they were at the barn that I drove up and checked the car and found nobody around.

Here was the game warden going up to check out what he thought was some "city" holiday travelers or berry pickers, that turned out to be armed robbers and murderers. Lucky or ...????

Always Forward

On this patrol it was the morning of a fresh snow. It was one of the first snows of the year that is really slippery and hard to drive on.

There was an area I wanted to check out for illegal activity back on some two-tracks. It was a rough area and put a patrol car to the test. I headed down the rutted trail, all the time going down a grade. After traveling for a while, I soon realized that I might have a problem on this wet, slippery snow. There was no way I was going to back out of this area up the grade I had been traveling down.

By now I had traveled a little farther down this trail than I had been before. But, no problem. I hated to back up and cover ground already traveled anyway. Onward I went. All of a sudden I came to a bridge. The bridge posed a little problem. It seems like when they pulled out of this area, after logging it off, they thought the planks off the bridge should go with them!

So, there I sat. I couldn't back up and didn't want to anyway. I couldn't go forward with a bridge that isn't a bridge anymore ahead of me. Or can I?? I pulled the car up to the bridge I-beams and got out. After a careful check of things, I figured that the wheels on the patrol car lined up about 2/3rds on the I-beams, so why not.

Real slowly I pulled onto the beams and headed across the hundred feet of the creek. About half-way across you all of a sudden get that feeling. Just maybe, you are not too bright, and this move may not go down in the same history books as the Lunar Landing, if you should slide off these beams.

But, I made it to the other side, so off I went on my patrol, only to find out that there was a reason the planks had been taken off the bridge. A short while later the two-track dead ended. If you think crossing that bridge the first time was stupid, scary, and not too bright, think about having to do it again on the way back.

One thing that for some reason never crosses a new game warden's mind is: Fresh snow on the ground this morning, checking out a two-track with no vehicle tracks in front of me and only one set behind me. (mine) Driving in type area nobody in their right mind would ever drive in, what in the world am I doing here in the first place!!

You Dummy ! Me!

The fall of the year is A crazy time for game wardens. You have everything going on at once. The fall fish runs, shining, waterfowl season, trapping, and all the normal calls an officer gets.

On this day I received word of some illegal traps set on muskrat houses out on a little lake west of town. I went out to this area to check things out.

After getting to the area from the back side, I put on my waders and headed out into the lake. Maybe a better way of putting it is a marsh with a lake for a name. The water, the first eighteen inches of which was mud, was up over my waist. I went to the first muskrat house I saw, and sure enough, I found three illegally set muskrat traps.

I continued around the lake and pulled two-three traps on each house. The mud and water all the time up over my waist right near the top of my boots. But, I kept right on going because I had always heard about this type violator, but never caught one.

It seems they would come into a lake or marsh area that held a good population of muskrats. They would then just set traps all over the houses and feed beds, illegally trapping out a lake in a twenty-four hour period. The traps were never marked, needless to say, and you only had a chance in a million of ever catching them. So, needless to say, I wanted ed to real bad!

After checking most of the lake and a little area off the lake itself, I was standing out in mud and water up to my armpits with fifty some traps on my shoulders, sweating like an overworked mule, and just maybe about as dumb as one! Then this thought went through my mind. You Dummy!! Here you stand in mud and water up to your neck, the weight of fifty traps on your shoulders, in the middle of nowwhere! If you trip and fall, and by now it was a project just walking, nobody will ever find you!! Smart Move!!

But, I did make it out of the marsh and returned that night to catch the two guys that had set all the traps.

Too Close To Heaven

In the flat-land, marsh country that I patroled, there seems to be a real advantage to building a nice little house up in the top of a big pine tree to help you watch the area you are hunting. (In Michigan it is illegal to hunt with a firearm from a tree.)

While on patrol with an ORV 4-wheeler, I saw tracks of another 4-wheeler going off across a marshy area. So, I followed them. This party had built a nice trail, a few bridges across wet areas, and had traveled it a number of times. After going a couple of miles, I saw where he turned off along a ridge. I parked my ORV and walked along his tracks.

After walking for a while, I came to an area on the top of the ridge that was spread out and flattened to a nice little high ground area. In the middle of this area was a bait pile, a fake deer standing there looking down a runway, and a 4-wheeler under a big pine tree!

I looked up in this big tree and saw a building sitting up in the branches. Or should I say, I saw an object sitting way, way up in this big pine tree in the branches. After checking out the ORV driver and talking to him, I figured it was time to head up towards heaven and see what was in this sky-blind. So off I went.

There were metal foot pegs in the Red Pine tree to climb up on. I climbed and rested, climbed some more and rested, and all of a sudden when about half-way to the blind thought, "You big dummy, (again?) if you fall out of this tree, you are dead when you hit the ground. Then our buddy standing down there is going to leave you there to rot!" But, I was half-way up, and he was watching, and game wardens are no cowards! Not too bright at times, but no cowards! Up, up I went.

I finally made it to the blind and checked it out. In it were lights, a stove, and all the nicer things of home. These were removed.

You asked how high up it was? While up in the tree blind looking around, I decided to take some pictures of the bait pile down on the ground. This, so I would have some pictures of it for evidence. I took out my little instamatic 35mm camera and took a number of pictures of the fake deer and bait pile.

Would you believe that this blind was so high up in the tree that when I had the pictures developed that the apples and other things in the bait-pile did not even show up!

I really think, if I had one, I could have parachuted out of this blind.

A Chevy could have driven out!

Chapter-7

Dedication

This book is dedicated to those I grew up with who never got the chance to enjoy all of life like I did. I often take a minute to stop and think, then thank the Good Lord for all He did for me. This article is written from an article that appeared in my home town paper. I still have it in my desk. (Article used with permission of A. P.)

Ontonagon Herald, Thursday July 20, 1967.

Vietnam Spreads Shadow Over Ontonagon

(Editor's note: Reprinted below in it's entirety, and through special arrangement with the Associated Press, is the feature story of the Ontonagon Vietnam War casualties that appeared in many of the country's major Sunday newspapers on July 9. Readers will find that this account differs in some respects from the story as it was published in daily papers in this area. The Herald copy includes some parts that were apparently deleted from the material issued to other papers, and it also includes the photographs that were taken here. Author of the story is AP News feature writer John Barbour, who spent several days here in May gathering material for the article.)

The AP Story: **"The Dead Come Home"** by John Barbour

Ontonagon, Mich. (AP) This is a quiet town, never so busy you can't hear the call of birds wheeling over the river, nor so empty you won't be recognized as a stranger or friend along the seven blocks of downtown.

It is a town where children grow free to wander woods and build campfires on the Lake Superior shore, where a school board member runs a pool room on River Street as a teenage club, where the weekly newspaper prints personal notes of thanks on the front page, where people know each other's license plates and family troubles, where Winter draws people together, piles driftwood on the beach, and drives 200 inches of snow at the land, and yields slowly to Spring.

Ontonagon is a quiet town, a long way from Vietnam.

But on a cold night in April, Vietnam came to Ontonagon with brutal swiftness. A military car made two stops. A dutiful hand knocked softly on two doors. The words were brief, the facts few.

Two of 10,000

They are only names on the long list of American dead in Vietnam that now totals over 10,000. But in this town of 2,500 where people pride themselves in knowing most everybody, they were much more than names. They were a polite boy and a laughing child, an ambitious teenager and a good friend. They were intimate parts of people's lives: Ernie, whose parents died in a plane crash when he was two, whose high spirits led him through the troubles of growing up to become a young man of drive and promise. Billy, whose father died when he was 15, whose quietness was a puzzle to some, and gentleness to others, whose first thought was always the welfare of a friend.

Because Ontonagon is a long way from the center of dissent and dissension, a long way from draft card burning and war protest, its feelings are never noted in headlines. But it is a town with a high sense of duty and pride. It measures its losses and its hurt personally.

So it was when Ernie and Billy were killed, and the word brought to their homes with all reasonable human speed by a military messenger who is somehow forgotten.

From those two centers of grief and dismay, like ripples on a darkened pond, the shock spread through the town, from family to family, from the mill to Stubb's Bar, by telephone and hushed word of mouth, ending always in frustrated, unbelieving silence.

First Casualty

The first Ontonagon boy to die in Vietnam came last June. Kenneth Somero, 24, a graduate of Ontonagon High School, was on a week end pass. He was shot by a sniper. "My God," said one townswoman, " What kind of war is it? You can't tell your friends from your enemies." It was a week between the first word that Billy and Ernie had been killed, and the arrival of their bodies in Ontonagon. In stunned silence of that week, most of the town came to grips with the reality.

For many, it was a time to count memories, and a time for anger and worry.

A mother who knew both boys found it hard to think about them with her own son waiting to be drafted. A mother with a boy already in Vietnam could no longer hide her personal terror. A usually quiet man where Billy had worked broke into an unexplainable meaningless fit of cursing one night in front of his friends. "Ontonagon only has 2,500 people, and it's lost three," said Mrs. Irene Wolfe, editor of the weekly Herald, "We have the feeling it isn't over yet."

Remembers Ernie

Mrs. Nancy Kulppi, who lives in Marquette now, but who grew up with Ernie Skinner, broke down when she heard the news. She remembered him as a talkative, laughing child with dark flashing eyes. In all sincerity he gave her a present once, wrapped in an old box. It was a dead frog he had found in the road. He was only four then. She was six, but she remembered.

And she remembered the silly, inconsequential things that made up their childhood together, making walkie-talkies with embroidery thread snitched from her mother, playing leapfrog over the tombstones in the cemetery, searching out the home of a favorite teacher and being too afraid to knock on the door, bicycling into town for the first time and getting lost on the backstreets of its smallness, taking forbidden swims in the lake, eating paid-for watermelon and stolen corn on the cob, camping overnight in the woods and making coffee with swamp water, and having to throw it out because it was full of frog's eggs.

When Nancy saw him in the open casket for the last time she thought, "He looked older and so tired," and she cried again. "I guess it was knowing my childhood was over," she said.

Knew both

Donald Roehm, 22, was working at the paper mill when he got the word Billy Lundberg was dead. It hit him hard. He owed his job to Billy who had stepped aside in the mill's seniority ranks and took a laboring job in those months before he was drafted to let Donnie have the better job as papertester Billy had been in line for.

When he left work, Donnie went to the Veterans of Foreign Wars Hall where his father tends bar. It was there he heard about Ernie who had been his best friend all through high school. In Donnie's words, he could not say, nor do a thing.

"The only thing I remember was disbelief," Donnie said, "until they brought the caskets home and I saw it was true with my own eyes."

Billie and Ernie formed two separate chapters in Donnie's life, Ernie in high school where he shared the principal's discipline for upsetting their classes, and where at least once Ernie had taken Donnie's share of the punishment.

Donnie looked far away, remembering. "He loved life so much, and he knew how to live it," he said, "and something like this has to happen before he had a chance."

After graduation, Ernie left town to learn the trade of meat cutting and to work in supermarkets in Illinois. Donnie became close then to Billy Lundberg, a quiet boy behind Donnie and Ernie in school.

The Dirty 30

They formed a post-high school group called "The Dirty Thirty" and even bought shirts with the name on it. They played pool together at the billiard parlor on River Street, and in league competition Donnie took first and Billy third. They held lawn parties and steak fries, and once a Christmas party with formal invitations to friends. They built a float for the Labor Day parade, a mechanized hand of a monster coming out of a box. It was called "The Thing", and it won first place.

But mostly Donnie remembers the long talks at night, sitting in the car, about the world, and girls, and their lives, and where they were going, and where they couldn't go.

"Billy was a type of kid you really had to get to know," Donnie said softly. "A lot of people thought he was quiet before they knew him better. In a crowd of guys, he didn't say much. He wasn't full of wise-cracks. He didn't say much around grownups either. He was always just polite."

Even weeks later, it was not easy for Donnie to talk about him, and he looked away as he did. "Billy'd never forget a friend," he said. "He cared about people and other people's feelings. And if we were ever in a jam, we stuck up for each other."

OHS Graduates

High School principal James Webber knew both the boys, and he heard the numbing news at home. "I came here in 1954, " he said slowly. "I had them in school for seven years."

They raise the flag at the high school at about 8:15 each morning, and it passes by Webber's second floor window on its way up, all 50 states and 13 colonies in star-spangled splendor. But Webber seldom sees it. His day starts early and busy, keeping his burgeoning school organized and disciplined for the job of teaching. Sitting in his crowded office behind his paperstacked desk, he thought back to the two boys.

"I probably knew Ernie better than Billy," he said. "He was a real spirited boy, and there were a lot of times I had him in the office here to talk turkey to him. But he was a good boy, too. He responded well, and grew into a responsible young man.

In fact, Ernie was a good friend of mine. At least, I felt so. He used to come here whenever he was back in town, and we'd talk about his job, and how he was getting along. Once he was worried about some people who worked for him, but were not doing their jobs. He felt he had to fire them in loyalty to his employer, but he didn't want to do it. And he was concerned about his friends here, that they weren't doing as much with their lives as they should. He was determined he was going to."

Raised By Grandparents

Ernie was raised by his grandparents. He called them mother and father, but they were older than most mothers and fathers. His grandmother, Mrs. Fay Noble, was the only white-haired member of the Kindergarten Mother's Club. She and her husband, who died in 1959, had one ambition: to see Ernie and his younger sister, Reba, graduate from high school. Mrs. Noble and Reba still live in the white frame home west of town, where Ernie grew up. Reba's husband, Tom, was brought home from military duty in Thailand for Ernie's funeral.

Ernie worked all through high school, first at Wager's Restaurant where the milk shakes are thick and a big sign on the wall proclaims, "Attention High School Students. Absolutely no smoking in this establishment or you will be asked to leave."

Later he worked at the IGA Foodliner where owner Henery Hoefferle remembers his ambition and his hard work. "We felt especially bad about it because he worked with us, and we knew what he was like," Hoefferle said standing at the check-out counter. "And when you lose two boys from a town as little as this—- that's sadness."

At the local chapter of the United Papermakers and Paperworkers Union, where Billy belonged, they draped the charter in black. And they remember things about him, his self-lessness, and how he lent money to a buddy to go to college even though he wasn't going himself.

Billy's mother, Mrs. Robert Letson, still can't bear to talk about her son's death. She has Billy's younger brother and sister, Freddie and Nyra, at home as well as two children from her present marriage. Billy's sister, Linda, was injured in an auto accident, coming to spend Mother's Day at home. In a town where not many people move away, Billy's family had lived here only ten years. They came from Green Bay, Wis. in 1957.

War Brought Home

The Rev. David Musall, pastor of St. Paul's Lutheran Church where Billy's family attended, recalled the disbelief that spread through the town.

'It isn't like World War II, when everybody was involved in some way," he said. "This war seemed so distant until something like this brought it home."

"But there are men in this town who have been in the service, who have seen things like this happen before," he said. "Maybe they wonder if there is as good a reason to fight now as when they fought. But, above it, they have a sense of national pride and duty."

As a minister in a town where trouble brings people closer together, he wondered what he should do if war struck one of the sons of his congregation, as he felt it would. He chose for the sermon at Billy's funeral, the 121st Psalm: " I will lift up mine eyes unto the hills, from whence cometh my help. My help cometh from the Lord.....The Lord shall preserve thy going out and thy coming in from this time forth, even for evermore."

For even in death, he reasoned, one must concern himself with the living and their consolation through faith in The Lord.

Ernie's Letter

The weekly Herald published again a letter it had printed three months earlier from a soldier in Vietnam. The writer had requested his name withheld. It was addressed to the people of Ontonagon, and said:

"The last couple of weeks I have seen notes in the paper about bringing our boys home."

"No man wants to leave home and go to war, but the great leaders of our country think we have to, to keep peace in our country. Every man that is here would like to be home, but we know we have to be here, and while we are here we are going to do our best to fight, and die, if we must, to keep our country free."

"We do not ask much of the people at home, just a little support will make it a lot easier, to know the people at home are pulling for us. We also feel we are winning the war, and we have a right to be here. Please do not protest the war."

This time the letter was signed, "Ernie Skinner."

Peace Group

A month after the letter first appeared, a panel of faculty members from Michigan Technological University in Houghton, some 60 miles away, gathered in Ontonagon to argue the Hawks and Doves viewpoints of the war. They met vocal opposition, some called it heckling, from a group of veterans in the audience.

The panel had been arranged in part by Mrs. Donald Archibald who heads a peace group in the county. She estimates the group's membership at between 25 and 30, one of them her husband, Dr. Donald Archibald, one of Ontonagon's three practicing physicians.

The group says that its purpose is to study the situation in Vietnam, "and it is the feeling of this group that we have no reason why we should have American military involvement in Vietnam, and that involvement is a great threat to world peace and carries with it the grave threat of a nuclear third world war."

The peace group finds little sympathy in Ontonagon. And throughout the period of mourning for Ernie and Billy, the group kept its silence.

"The two didn't use any politics, any Vietnam pro and con," said one veteran who believes in the U.S. presence in Southeast Asia. "They just thought of the two boys.... Funny thing, I haven't heard anyone criticize the war. I think if they had, I'd have spoken up."

One veteran of a bigger, older war felt anger when he heard about the efforts of heavyweight champion Cassius Clay to avoid military service.

"Here's a guy who made a fortune out of this country.... who really had a chance to be real popular, but then who did this thing," he said with disgust. "And here's two kids who never had a chance."

Varied Reactions

But mostly the reactions were more gentle than that. One old man, his eyes glistening in the sun, leaned across the breakfast room table in the home he built and remembered the little boy, "I bounced on my knee." Another old man who knew one of the boys well broke into uncontrollable tears at the funeral home and had to be helped outside. One teacher found a desk in her classroom with the name "Ernie Skinner" carved in it, and another found some old test papers the boys had done in school. One man remembered how Ernie on his last visit home had confided that someday he wanted to put a proper marker on his parents' grave in Oregon.

These were things the townspeople remembered, quietly, each in his own way. The bodies came home separately. A military guard of honor accompanied them. Flowers were sent from Vietnam, from the men of Company B, Fourth Battalion, 23rd Infantry, 25th Infantry Division, the final buddies of Ernie and Billy. All the businesses in town closed in their honor. The veterans without any formal organization quickly posted an honor guard for each boy. The men stood short tours, passing on and wearing one tired VFW hat whether they were members or not.

How It Happened

What the town didn't know, except for rumor, was how the boys had died. Considering the shock the town endured, perhaps it was just as well, because they had died as they had lived.

Their company was on patrol in the heavily forested area near CuChi, some 25 miles northwest of Saigon. They came under heavy fire from Viet Cong guerrillas. One Sergeant saw three of the enemy running into the underbrush and gave chase. He didn't come back.

Sgt. Ernie Skinner started out to look for him. He had moved barely 15 yards when a burst of enemy automatic weapons fire cut him down. Corp. Lundberg saw him hit, leaped from his position and firing his 25-pound M-60 machine gun as he charged, ran toward the enemy line. Another burst from the concealed enemy position hit him and he slumped to the ground. When the battle was over, they were found in the brush only a few feet apart.

Lundberg was awarded the Silver Star, and Skinner the Bronze Star, both posthumously.
The town wondered what fate had taken these two boys from them, two boys so unalike, who knew each other only casually at home. What had brought them to Vietnam, and to the same company, and the same patrol, and the same moment of death, both victims of their own bravery and self-sacrifice.

They were brought back to be buried. And Nancy Kulppi remembered how she and Ernie had run home from the cemetery one night, frightened by a ghostly clinking noise in the wind. The next day they had laughed when they found it was only the flag clips blowing against the pole. Now Ernie is buried barely 15 feet from the same flagpole in the same cemetery.

And a man who knew Billy, and how close he had been to his father, remembers how hurt Billy had been when his father died. And now Billy lies by his father's side in another cemetery in another town.

My thoughts

I just wanted you to get a chance to read this article that may let you feel the heart and soul of the people that make up the U.P.

When I was growing up, a small town (Ontonagon) in the U.P. was a family. Everybody knew everybody, helped everybody when a need arose, and everybody hurt with everybody when something happened. I hope you can feel this through Mr. Barbour's article. I could never put a small town's feelings into words like he did.

In a way, this time period affected all our lives. Some of us were just able to make it through this time into our dreams, while others had their lives cut short. I have used the story about Billy and Ernie dozens of times when talking to youth groups about how important having character is.

How small is the U.P.? I have in front of me an article from the Ontonagon Herald. It reads in part: William Raymond Lundberg..... born in Manistique, Mi., July 31,1946. His grandmother was Mrs. Cecil Gonders of Cooks, Mi. This is the area where I lived and worked for the last 20 years.

I sit here and recall many a basketball game with Billy at the old tennis courts back home. And going out to Ernie's, turning after the Norwich Road and going on up the hill.......

The Boy-Men of Vietnam

I will close this chapter with this last, old yellowed newspaper article from my desk, written by the Editor of the Tuscola County Advertiser: From there, through a letter home, this Marine PFC has helped me to better understand the beardless men of Vietnam.

If there is such a thing as an average GI, what's he like? Well, in most cases he is unmarried. His only material possessions of value are an old car at home and a transistor radio over there. His world is filled with ugly smells, and rock music, loud laughter and 105mm howitzers and sometimes sobbing.

He's just out of school, received so-so grades, played a little football, and has a girl who promised to be true and who writes a letter......sometimes.

He has learned to swagger, swear, and drink beer, because it is cool, and it is the thing for a boy-man to do.

He's a PFC with a year in and one to go, or maybe three.

Back home he worked only when he had to. He preferred waxing his own car to washing his dad's, but he works now. From dawn to dark, every minute he's not fighting, he's working. It sure beats thinking.

He can dig a foxhole, first aid a wounded buddy, march until told to stop or stop until told to march. He has stood among hills of bodies and helped to build some of those hills, and when somebody died he knew, he cried and cried.

The boy who littered his backhome room with soiled stuff for Mom to pick up now has two pair of fatigues; he wears one while he washes the other. He sometimes forgets to clean his teeth, but never his rifle. He will share his water with anybody who is thirsty, split his rations with anybody hungry, and throw half his ammo to you if you are fighting for your life.

He does the work of three civilians, draws the pay of one, yet finds ironic humor in it all.

He learns to fight with his hands and his weapons as his hands. He is pinked-cheeked, tousle-haired, tight-muscled, 18 years old fighting to make 19, then he's 19 fighting to make 20. He's scared.

He doesn't understand fighting no-win wars in unpronounceable places with less than our best weapons, with the fat targets off limits. He doesn't understand killing Communists in Vietnam, when we tolerate them in Cuba.

So he grumbles, sometimes.....

But then he gets a night's rest and a letter from home and returns from a paddy patrol still forked-end down and he is lucky. And as he closes his eyes and thanks God and says a prayer....... for us back home.................
A GI

Illegal Rifle

Chapter-8
Grandpa's Big Buck

I have told people over and over that storytelling like I grew up with is becoming a lost art. It seems like now most hunting camps have a TV and microwave. Back when I was a kid, all camps had was a wood stove and some great stories.

This is one my dad told to me at least a zillion times. Why? It was about his dad and his big buck.

You have to remember back in my growing up days there were a lot of big bucks around. I tell people that they would not believe some of the deer I saw. But, nobody ever kept a rack from a buck. They were nailed to the side of the old outbuilding till they fell off and the mice ate them. I sometimes wish we had kept a few just to let people know what the racks were like. This one was kept.

As the story goes, it seems that Grandpa was going back into hunting camp using a team of horses and a jumper. He left the farm on the Norwich Road and headed off across the field. His plans were to cut through the woods toward the old potato fields, hit the Main Line, and go back into camp.

(I can picture this area in my mind just like Dad and I were once again walking down the trail, and he was once again pointing out what took place.)

As he stood on the jumper driving the team of horses, he came to a little swale (wet, muddy area) where there was a lot of small, finger size brush and Aspen growing. There was snow on the ground so it was easy going and easy to see.

As Grandpa went through this swale, he looked off over the head of the right horse of the team, and standing in the middle of some of this brush was one of the nicest bucks he had ever seen. He pulled back on the reins, real easy, to bring the horses to a stop. Here he stood on the jumper now looking right between the ears of the right hand horse at this big buck, just standing in the brush looking at him.

Grandpa had his 30-30 Winchester lying across his arms, where he always carried it when driving the team. He knew with the barrel pointing to the left, he would have to slowly bring it all the way around, and turn just a little. But, he also knew that most of his actions were hidden behind the horse that was standing between him and the buck.

He got his gun swung around, turned just a little and all this time held firm pressure on the reins that were wrapped around his arms so the horses would not move. Grandpa stood there watching this monster buck knowing all the time that if he moved too much it would be off through the brush before he could get a shot at it.

Slowly he brought his 30-30 up behind the horse, a little higher right behind the horse's head, till he had it aimed between the horse's ears, right at the big buck. Grandpa knew it was now or never, and this buck was a dandy even back in those days. But should he shoot at it like this?

Finally he had a perfect shot at the buck, right over the horse's head, between its ears. He slowly pulled the trigger.

The next thing he knew his arm was about jerked off and the horses were running wide open down the trail with Grandpa trying to stay on the jumper and keep from being dragged to death!

He finally got the horses to settle down and stop. Then Grandpa started to check all his body parts to see if they were all still attached. He was not sure that the arm that had the reins wrapped around it was not now about a foot longer than his other arm. At least it sure felt this way.

But, after things calmed down, Grandpa turned the horses around and went back to the area of the swail where the big buck had been standing. There lay Grandpa's big buck that was going to be talked about for years to come. He was not even sure he had hit it, he had left the area so fast, but he had.

Hunting camp tales, they never die, they just get better as the years go by. Throw out the TV and sit down with the grandkids and tell them a few, so they have something to pass on to their kids.

Chapter-9
My Opinion (1)

Dear Editor:

This is an article I wrote for the local paper about the wrong attitude that is so often given out about deer hunters.

I am a retired Michigan Conservation Officer that has now written three books about working as a game warden and growing up in the back-woods of the U.P. As I travel around with these books I get to talk with hundreds and hundreds of people while attending book signings and booths at outdoor shows. Over and over I hear, "Where is the problem?" or "Is the DNR causing people to think there is a problem where there is not one?" For this reason I stopped at a DNR office and got some information and wrote this article.

I sure hope you will print it in either the outdoor section or as a letter to the Editor.

Sincerely: John A. Walker

Well, here we are into another new year. Time goes so fast when you're having fun it is really hard to believe. I guess I should just start the new year out right and add fuel to the fire.

First of all, let me tell you a tale about myself, and I'm sure there are a few other fathers out there that have been there. One time as my kids were growing up, it was report card time. The kids brought their report cards home, and one of them came in to show theirs to Dad. I was sit-ting in the living room and looked the card over. It was a real good report card, mostly "A's", a "B" or two, and one "C" in math. As I looked over the report card I mentioned the "C" and how we would have to work a little harder on that subject.

A little while later, while still sitting in my chair, I overheard my child in the kitchen talking to her Mom about the report card.. I never forgot what was said because of the way it was said. "Mom, didn't Dad like all the "A's" and "B's" on my report card?" Even a "Yooper" did not have to be too smart to understand he blew it by talking only about the one grade that should be worked on without telling about the 99% that were excellent.

I think there are a whole lot of others in this world that make the same mistake. Let me explain.

First, let me say that the deer hunters of the U.P. had maybe better place an ad in the lost and found section of their local papers for their State Senator, State Representative, and U.S. Congressman. I think most of these got lost when it came to standing up for the hunters on the deer blind issue.

I have always felt that as a group, the deer hunters of Michigan are some of the best behaved people there are, so I started out to collect some facts to prove my point.

(1) In the last year I could get figures for, there were 107,000 deer hunters in the U.P. During the time when all these 107,000 hunters seem to want to be in the same place at the same time there were only 72 complaints received on these 107,000 hunters. Now, some of you that are a whole lot smarter than me, try to figure out if this is a problem. When you figure out what the percentage is you will see what I mean, and then place it on a graph!!! It will not even show up to the human eye!!

Now, don't get me wrong. I'm not saying there are not some jerks out there because we all know there are, but please don't paint all of us with the same brush.

I was told that the figure for the number of hunters this year in the U.P. should top the 107,000 mark, and there were only 54 complaints recorded according to the article I read in the paper. This tells this "Yooper" that not only were there more hunters, but they were even better behaved. If this is true, how come in papers and on TV all during deer season, all we saw and read was about the problems with hunters, their blinds and their baiting? Something just does not figure out. If, and I say if, all of these problems were blind and bait related, and they were not, you still do not have a problem like some people would make you think there is.

(2) While traveling back from Florida at Christmas time, I was listening to a news article, not a sports show, but the normal news. They were talking about how deer hunting is one of the safest sports there is today. By our Federal government's own statistics on outdoor activities, hunting rates safer than- **Get ready**- fishing, boating, and golf!! There must be some real problems on those golf courses!! Not only did I, but the people on the radio station, found these facts rather interesting.

(3) I was also told that the reason blinds (as 99% of us use them) were outlawed was because someday someone could get hurt or even shot over a deer blind! OK, if they want to operate on this premise, let's outlaw public schools, gas stations, and banks, where people are shot across the country all the time. What they are trying to do does not hold water.

(4) Why are deer hunters treated differently than all the other sportsmen in the state? A duck hunter can build a waterfowl blind on State or Federal property and that is all right. Just place your name and address on it and remove it after season. A fisherman can place an ice fishing shanty out on a lake just so he places his name and address on it and removes it after the end of season. You can even place a tent or house trailer out on State land if you post your name and address and remove it after so many days. Why, if all this is true, are they treating deer hunters differently? I don't think any of us have a problem with placing our name and address on our blinds, that should be of a portable nature, and removing them after the hunting season is over. But!! the way the X-DNR director had the law passed is anti-family and honest hunter. If you talk to anybody that really likes the outdoors and likes to hunt they laugh at this idea of taking a blind in and out of the woods each morning and night.

(5) The person that is writing this is a person who, when he was working and saw the type blinds, plus the mess some people were making, went to the U.S. Forest Service Office and asked the Federal Forest Supervisor if he wanted some tickets issued to those that I knew had built the blinds, then left them with their mess. I was told that it was not a problem, don't worry about it, and not a ticket was ever issued. I ask you, why was not the problem attacked by taking care of the problem blinds and letting the honest, respectful hunter enjoy his hunt?

I have to ask all you out there, why are they trying to make the size problem out of the deer blind issue they are? Their own facts don't justify it and there are those in their own department that cannot figure out the how and why of their attitude. Just maybe they were not lucky enough to overhear the talk from the kitchen like I did and learn a lesson.

In closing, I might suggest that if those whom you hunters are looking for in the lost and found are not located before deer season next year, they are sure to show up the week before, say about the 6th of November, and I'm sure you can find them then.

Chapter-9
My Opinion (2)

Well, it must be blast off time again! Fasten your seat belts, put some velcro on your seat, and listen to an old man's impressions.

Having grown up in "Yooper" land, the good old U.P., I always figured a paradox was a couple of wood ducks sitting on a log in the spring making googly eyes at each other. But, with all I have been reading in articles about baiting and those wanting to outlaw it, I think I have found out what it really is.

First: There are just too many "exspurts" running around in this day and age. I don't care what the subject is or what is taking place, there is someone or a group of someones who are "exspurts" on the subject! Do you realize how many of these "exspurt" type people that are trying to figure out our hunting and fishing rules never hunted or fished in their life? **BUT!** They are the "exspurts" in their field of study. Never having spent day after day out in the woods, never having sat in a deer blind, never took some youth out hunting or fishing with them, never got skunked but still had a great day, but they are the exspurts in the how and why of things. Why? Because they read some books and sat in some classes taught by another "exspurt" on the subject that just had it passed along to him. Where in the world is the old "on the job" taught "exspurt" that was field trained, not having just book learning? Give us outdoor people a break, please.

Second: Another case of "exspurts"! In my life time I have owned over fifty firearms at one time or another. Yet, never once did one of the guns that I owned say, "I guess I'll just go out and shoot someone tonight." A gun is a piece of metal, wood, and maybe some plastic that has no capability on its own to do such a thing. Let's stop and think and stop blaming the guns owned by honest people for the lack of character on the part of certain human beings. The "exspurts" blame it on the guns. The people that use their heads blame it on the person behind the gun. Don't throw all us hunters that have worked hard all our lives, raised our children to be an active part of society, love our nation and what it stands for, into the crowd that would drive by a house and empty a gun at it! I think the hunters of our nation are getting a bum rap from the "exspurts" once again.

The Third case of the "exspurt": I guess this is the worst one of the three; this is the "exspurt-paradoxer"! This is the "exspurt" that goes out to talk to the local farmer and sees that he has some serious crop damage on his farm. So he gives him a permit to cut down on the deer herd on and around his farmland. "Too many deer" our "exspurt" says. **BUT!** Then he goes and talks to a sportsmen's group and says, "Yup, the deer herd seems to be way down, I guess this is caused by the little old man sitting in his deer blind over a bucket of apples! So, let's stop baiting for deer." Therefore the taking of less deer, therefore an increase in the deer herd to go into this farmer's field to cause more crop damage, therefore a need to increase the farmer's crop damage permits, to take more deer the sportsman could have taken. I call this the voice of the "exspurt-paradoxer"!!

I have always threatened to have a chapter in one of my books on how to convince these "exspurts-paradoxers" from the government side at a public hearing. It would consist of about five blank pages, because usually their minds are already made up by the "exspurts" long before they ever call for a public hearing on a subject. How in the world can a person ever hope to change the mind of an "exspurt-paradoxer" of their opinion of how things should be?

I guess our only hope is that someday those two wood ducks that make up an "exspurt-paradoxer" will fall off their log and some with a good "Yooper" mentality will crawl up on the log and take their place.

Chapter-9
My Opinion (3)

Well, a lot of those people out there that read the Fish Report heard for the first time last week that their deer blinds are going to outlawed. They are not too happy to say the least. I received a good number of calls and had over a dozen people ask me on the street about it. The DNR is not going to score many points with the average person with this move. This kind of leads into the question I have been asked at least a zillion times in the last two weeks, "What do you think of the split in the DNR?" Let me make a couple of points.

1) I have made it a point to talk to DNR people I come across in my travels from one side of the U.P. to the other. (Even some downstate.) Of all I have talked to, from a number of divisions, I have yet to come across one that does not think the split may be a good idea. There are those I talked to that are worried about the effect this split may have on their job, if they are still going to have one, but the idea that the DNR has gotten too big and too involved in too many things they agree with.

2) The scary part is the power given to one person in leadership of the DNR. This seems to scare most people, and the deer blind issue brought it to the surface. When the DNR is no longer really run by a commission, and the Director, whoever it may be, has sole power to pass laws and rules to his feelings and his whims, all the people in the state of Michigan are in trouble. I believe our forefathers maybe had some wisdom when they placed checks and balances within a system. It was never meant that a governor could place his personal man in a position where he had sole power to control the system. I had an older party tell me just this morning, "John, I really think we are losing our rights as people one little step at a time till we won't have any anymore someday." In a proper system, everybody has to be accountable to someone.

3) It seems that so many people want to get back to the "Good Old Days" of the Conservation Department. Their feeling is that the average person had more input within the system during those days. It seems to all boil down to what I have been trying to say in the last couple of weeks. The big problem is, we can never return to the **"Good Old**

Days". It just won't happen. Thinks have changed too much, and there are too many special interest groups all trying to get their personal points across.

I explain to people that ask me this way. "We all know of someone that hits forty and decides he missed something back around seventeen. So, he leaves his wife and kids and goes back to his teenage years looking for it. Needless to say, he never finds it, for life has moved on during this time."

The split may be a good thing for the people of Michigan, but we are never going to return to life as it was back in the forty's and fifty's. Life just does not work this way.

4) The other thing I hear from within and outside the DNR is that maybe this split will help the DNR to regain some of the rapport with the average hunter and fisherman in the state. I personally think they are dreaming. If the way the same people who are going to be the leadership of the "New" DNR handled the baiting and deer blind issue is any example of how they are going to operate, it will be business as usual, and all the average hunters and fishermen are in trouble. **Still!!**

In other words, for things to work out like a lot of people would like to see them, there has to be a lot more done then just a split and the closing of some offices. I feel there has to be some accountability back to the people by those that are placed in leadership of some of the key organizations of the state. The "New" DNR commission has to be non-political and made up of people that love and understand the proper use of the great outdoors by all those that love it, not just the people or special interest groups that make the most noise. The director of the "New" DNR also has to be accountable and not have total power with no checks or balances.

This is just one "Yooper's" opinion, and I already have been told what it is worth.

Chapter-9
My Opinion (4)

I am sitting here on the one and only April Fool's Day of 1996, BUT what I am going to tell you is totally true. The article was out in the news this past weekend and on the radio this morning, April 1.

For you that are against hunting animals, get ready! I have always said this day would come, and it did! This summer one of the animal rights groups is going after sport fishermen! They are going to start protesting the right to fish and plan to disrupt fishermen's activities. **Can you believe it!! Humans are nuts!!**

In a more serious nature, please let me point something out.

This winter may go down in history as one of the worst in years for deer lost due to starvation. Some figures I have heard run to 250 thousand deer or more. Please let me point something out.

For you who are against hunting because it is "cruel", maybe you should take a ride out into the deer yards after the snow melts. It's funny in a way, but the "Nature" way of taking care of things is one of the "cruelest" you will ever see.

In all the years I have spent out in the woods both working and on my own, plus with all the people I have come across in my travels, there have been a number of times I have witnessed "Nature's" way of doing things.

In my travels, I have observed where the raccoons get over-populated in an area, then "Nature" comes along, and they get what we call distemper. With this, they seem to lose it, they wander around circles, stumble around, foaming at the mouth, dying a slow, agonizing death. If you had received all the calls from people that had these raccoons in their yards, and didn't understand what was going on, you would know what I mean.

Closer to home, we all seem to understand that the deer herd has exploded in the last few years. I can remember sitting in my blind and thinking it was a great evening if you saw two, three deer moving around.

But, in the same blind ten years later, I would lose count of all the deer moving around. At times it looked like the whole woods had movement in it at one time. As hunters and sportsmen try to manage wildlife along with the agencies involved, whether it be deer or anything else, the anti-hunters come out of the woodwork.

It may sound funny, but I think at times both sides misunderstand "Nature". Some want to stop hunting altogether, while others want to only shoot big bucks. I think both are wrong.

Here we are with a deer herd way too large for the area that has to support it. With the herd all out of proportion, you get a weaker herd. There is too much inbreeding in the herd. The strain of deer are smaller and not as healthy. So what happens? "Nature" comes along and takes care of the problem in His way.

We have snow from October till May?. The snow is deep and the weather is cold for month after month. What happens? The deer herd gets hit hard, and between a quarter and a half million deer may die!

Is this bad? Yes and no. We all hate to see starvation and the hard way deer die during a long hard winter, but the ones that die are the small, weak, and sickly of the deer herd. "Nature's" way of doing things.

But! What is left? The strong, healthier animals of the herd, and this is not all bad. From these animals that are left you will get a better strain of deer. Is it cruel? Is "Nature's" way wrong? Who am I to say?

But! I do think we have to have a good sound management program. This program should have input by both the public and the expert. The surplus of fish, birds, and animals should be harvested and made use of. It has to be a good sound program with all factors put into the equations. I think government agencies have to get back in touch with people on the street, or should I say, the average person out in the woods. I think people have to be re-taught the value of good, sound wildlife management.

Please stop and think:

A total protection of hawks, owls and other predators and the partridge, sharptail, and other small animals pay.

Protest trapping and stop it, then beaver populations get out of control, and we lose thousands of board feet of lumber and other valuable trees.

I could go on and on, but what I am trying to say is that managed hunting, trapping, and other controls are needed. If not, don't cry when "Nature" takes over and solves the problem.

Illegal Pike

Chapter-10
Judges Make For Interesting People

Some of my favorite people have been judges. It is interesting to think back after you have worked for 25 years with all kinds of them. I thought you may like to hear a few tales about how creative an officer has to be with some of the judges they end up having to work with.

I always had an opinion that when growing up, the youth who was walked back and forth to school everyday by his mother, spent all the time at recess doing his school work, never went out and got dirty, never pulled a girl's pigtail, never pulled one of those pranks all youth pull, grew up to be a lawyer. As fate would have it, later this same party managed to be elected judge.

Now, don't misunderstand me. There are also judges who are rather interesting as far as conservation law violators go. There was one at one time, that if he could, he would have taken everything used in the crime down to the violator's BVD's, and sent them home in these, on foot.

There was another court in the county I bordered downstate that had this saying when the pheasants became really scarce. When a party was caught taking pheasants illegally, in the same area where other crimes were laughed at, the saying went like this: "Take a pheasant go to jail, rob a gas station get probation".

Some Judges' Tales:

Where There's A Will, There's Always A Way

In one of the areas that I worked with, there was this rather interesting judge. He was really a good guy, but never hunted or fished, so he knew absolutely nothing about it. He was totally confused when you tried to talk to him about shining, illegal hunting, or illegal fishing. **But,** he was a lover of the outdoors and walked out in the woods all the time watching birds, studying flowers, etc . **So,** the officers had to work around their problem.

One night we were sitting in the lane between a couple of corn fields. There was a little hill here where we could sit and watch the road both ways. As we sat, a car approached from our right using a spotlight to shine. We stayed where we were hiding till the car went by us and continued down the road.

We only had one problem. In this area where we were working the roads were all real straight, and it was hard to drive without lights on account of all the traffic. I thought for a minute then told my partner, "Plug in that spotlight off the back floor and shine it out your window." He did, and here we went down the road after the car we wanted to check shining just like they were. When we got close enough to stop them, we shut off the hand-held spotlight, turned on the blue light and spotlights, and pulled up behind their car.

They did not stop, but sped up down the gravel road. As we followed them, they threw out a firearm and some other objects, then pulled over and stopped. After recovering the spotlight and getting some identifiaction from them, we walked back up the road to see what they had thrown out.

Here we found a rifle and two clips full of rifle shells. We had a good case, right? We had observed them using a spotlight to shine for deer, they had a rifle and shells in their car, what else could we ask for? Wrong! We were in the area with a judge who did not know anything about night hunting. Did not want any cases brought before him on it. So what could we do?

I got to thinking. Now, if what we would like to issue them a ticket for will not work, how about a ticket for littering. This the judge could understand, and I knew he was a stickler about this.

So, we made out the tickets for littering a public road with one 30-06 rifle and two clips loaded with 30-06 shells.

The judge really understood how dangerous this could be, especially after I explained to him. "Your Honor, in the area where this firearm was thrown out, there are a number of youth that have to walk down the edge of the road to catch the school bus on the corner. Now if they had found this rifle and shells laying along the edge of the road, one of them could have easily gotten hurt or maybe even killed!.."

He threw the book at them because this he could understand.

Don't Say That!

In this area there was a lot of pike spearing that took place in the spring of the year as they ran up the creeks to spawn. It had become a real problem with teenagers that were old enough to drive, but not old enough for "real" court. In other words the judge felt they were adults in some areas, but not in others.

On this evening we ran into a crew of youth from one of the better know families of outlaws. They had been hard at work, and their luck had been better then average. They had about half a gunny sack full of nice pike they had speared. I knew right away I was between a rock and a hard spot on what to do.

But, I felt I should do something so I issued them all tickets for spearing pike illegally.

I knew from having traveled down the road before with this crew that the fireworks had yet to start. On the day for court, I was all ready. I had the spears, the lights they had used, and the frozen Northern Pike.

Court started out real smooth, but I soon found out that our judge must have gotten out on the wrong side of the bed that morning. The only good thing was when he landed, he landed on our side of things. When he finished tearing into these teenagers for what they had done, we still had to face their defense attorney!! **Their Mother!!!**

One thing I had gotten used to was the fact if you ran into any of this tribe, from nine to ninety, you had better be ready to put up with Mom coming into court with them to let you know what she thought of things. Today was no different.

When the judge got done, mother started in. The judge and all the rest of us just sat there as she gave us her opinion of the officers, the courts, and anything else she wanted to let fly at. As she finally began to tire and her closing remarks were coming to a close, she said, "And judge! I would sure like to know! What happens to all those nice pike?"

As the judge woke up and returned to life, (He had been one of the first judges appointed by Moses in the book of Exodus) he looked this lady right in the eye and said, "I hope to tell you, ma'am, these officers and their families have to eat too! So I'm sure the pike will be put to good use!"

I was sitting there about to croak! This was the last thing I wanted to hear, because this is what they all figured was true to start with. And really, it's not that way at all. You give them to a "needy" family, and then have them invite you over for supper.

This mother had by now just about gone ballistic! She knew she had finally heard the truth in court!

The judge just sat there till she settled down, then as calm as could be said, "Court adjourned." Got up and walked out.

You Know It And I Know It

On this day, I was on patrol in an area of a big waterfowl refuge. The first part of each waterfowl season, this place was a real zoo. There were hunters standing shoulder to shoulder and cars and campers parked all over the place. On this day it was no different.

I had been walking along the dikes checking hunters and watching the ducks fly in and out of the refuge. And laughing. It did not take the ducks long to learn that as you came to the edge of the refuge itself, you fast climbed to 10,000 feet, leveled off, flew to the corn field you wanted, and dropped straight down into it. Needless to say, the ratio of shots fired to ducks gotten was about a zillion to one.

Also needless to say, after you had spent all day working up here so you could check early shooters before daylight and late shooters after dark, you were beat. I got home to crash on the couch hoping I would be recovered enough to head back up to the refuge in the morning before daylight.

Wouldn't you know it, about 8:45pm I received a phone call that one of the county cars had a vehicle stopped with fresh blood all over the trunk. To top it off, the place where they were was about as far as you could travel in my area and still be in it, but off I went.

When I arrived, a county and city police car had a vehicle stopped with two youth in it. They told me what they had, and after we figured it out, we came to the conclusion we had nothing but a bloody trunk.

But, we also had our wit to try to outwit them. I got a little evidence kit out of the trunk and walked up to their car. We got the two subjects out and had them stand by the car. I then put on some rubber gloves, took a little scraper and a couple of glass vials out of the evidence kit and started to collect hair and blood samples from their trunk and back bumper. We then took a camera and took a number of pictures of the trunk area. After all this valuable evidence was collected, we went over to talk to the two subjects.

In a round about way, they were told that the evidence that had been collected was going to be sent to the state lab at Rose Lake. Here they would test the blood and hair we had collected and send the following information back to us. (1) Verify that it was deer's blood. (2) Tell us what sex deer had been killed. (3) Let us know about what time the deer had been shot.

After explaining to them what all was going to take place, we asked them if they knew what could be done with hair and blood samples. Did you ever see what they could do with them on TV? After thinking a minute, they both agreed they were had, so they admitted they had shot a small doe that evening. But, they would not tell us where the deer was now.

Back in those days, with a case like this you could just call the Justice of the Peace at home where his office was. Then, take the subjects over there. This we did, and about thirty minutes later, we were all standing in the local judge's back porch office.

We told him what we had found, that they had admitted they had shot a small doe, but we did not have the deer.

The JP asked the two young men what they had in mind, and they started to play word games with him. All of a sudden our judge said, "Hold it right there!! I know both you boys. Now, I know you shot that deer! The officers know you shot a deer! And most important, you both know you shot a deer! Illegally! Now you have fifteen minutes to leave this office, go pick up that deer, and be back here with it! **Now get!!**"

Off they went. The JP then looked at all of us standing there and said, "You know you have a pretty weak case on these two without the deer, don't you?" This was no surprise to us. We had known it all the time, and so did the judge who had been a police officer himself at one time.

The two subjects returned about ten minutes later with a deer and, stood before the local JP who took care of the matter.

By the way, back in those days and unless things have changed since I retired, you might be able to do item one, a check for deer blood, but item two and three could only be done on TV and at the movies. Not in real life.

I guess some people just watch too much TV.

Chapter-11
Lucky Me? (1)

This is a collection of tales that for some reason those who starred in them wish they had never taken place. But, they sure are fun to tell and retell.

I Sure Wish I Hadn't Done That

Well, I guess whenever a couple hunters, fishermen, or any outdoor lovers get together they have to tell tales on each other. This is one I heard at an outdoor show the other day. Whenever these stories are floating around I always tell people, "They have to be true because we all know hunters and fishermen don't lie! Right?" You should see some of the looks I get when I tell people this. This is one of those "true" stories told on a buddy.

It seems that there was this group of guys that got together to go on a fishing trip. The area where they were going was way up north and kind of remote. The fishing was great, and the time together in the great outdoors was a ball. It seems in the area where they were fishing there were a good number of black bear. The owner of the resort told them to just leave the cubs alone and stay away from Mom.

One day while out fishing along a stream, in the area where there were a ton of wild blueberries, they came across a mother bear with three cubs. The mom took off cross country with two of the cubs in tow, while the third cub went up the first tree it came to as fast as it could climb. There was one guy (there is always one in each group) in this group of fishermen that just wanted to catch a bear cub. Seeing mother had hightailed it through the woods with the other two cubs, our fisherman set down his pole on the creek bank and started up the tree after this cub.

Now, if you have ever watched a cub bear when it is scared, it will climb all the way to the very top of a tree up on the smallest limb trying to get away. Right after this cub came our now brave fisherman knowing the sow bear was gone. Brave,seeing mom was gone and it was him against the cub. Up and up they went till they were right to the very top of the tree!

Our fisherman came up behind the cub within reach of it, just below it. He then reached up to grab it by the hind leg. As he got hold of the cub's hind leg, he got a firm grip and started to pull on the cub. The cub started crying like crazy as the fisherman tried to pull it loose from the tree. All of a sudden our fisherman found out that the biting end of a bear cub is not all you have to worry about!!

Here came the bear cub's other defense! Recycled blueberries and all!! All of a sudden our big brave fisherman did not have any desire to capture this bear cub anymore. Down the tree he came in about three giant steps! He hit the ground running, and went off the bank, face first in the water to wash off! As his buddies about died rolling on the ground laughing at what they had just watched take place.

Score, bear cub one-fisherman zero!

Chapter-11
Lucky Me? (2)

But! But! Officer.....

I guess I have to tell this tale about having a super "Yooper" bad day that only went from bad to worse.

It seems that there was this big outdoor show that was to be held up in the "Yooper" dome. This is just about ninety miles from home base. Now, if you have ever taken part in something like this, it is a real zoo trying to move everything to the area of the show and getting it all ready to set up. It is a mad dash when the doors open so those with displays can get in and set up. For this big show, there were dozens of boats to move from your dealership to the show. One thing about pulling boats is that even a good "Yooper" can usually only pull one at a time. You have the boats to haul, all the display items, plus all the things to dress up your area trying to get folks to stop and look your boats over. When this is being done, everybody gets drafted to help out hauling things to the show. Family, friends, workers, even those that are not really too excited about helping get hauled into it.

Now, it seems that this one dealer had a real sharp used boat that was taken in on trade for a couple of 4-wheelers the fall before. Our dealer figured they would clean the boat up and place it in the show to try to sell it. The party setting up the show and displays got hold of one of the other people drafted into hauling boats the ninety miles up to the dome for them. He told him, "Hook onto that Bayliner boat we took in on trade last fall and haul it up here." He was asked, "Which boat is it?" He was told what make it was plus, "It's the only Bayliner that we have out in the yard, so you should have no problem finding it." Off went our reluctant boat hauler out to hook up to this used boat for the ninety mile trip up to the outdoor show.

As our reluctant boat hauler pulled into the parking area at the dome to drop the used boat off for the show, the party in charge of setting up the display for the dealership about died! It seems like those famous words we all use, "You should have no problem" didn't happen. He took one look at the reluctant hauler and said, "Man! That's not the boat I want! It's not even ours! It's not the one I wanted! This boat belongs to another party that just stored it at our place for the winter!"

Now our reluctant boat hauler is a super reluctant boat hauler, because he has to make the ninety mile trip back to home base with the wrong boat, hook up to the right boat, and make the ninety mile trip back, before making the final ninety mile trip back home for the night. What a day it has been already! It sure could not get any worse, **wanna bet!!**

As our super reluctant boat hauler is making the trip back with the wrong boat, it turns dark out. The lights on the boat trailer have the wrong hookup so are not working, so guess who pulls right up behind our reluctant boat hauler? You guessed it!! The officer stops our buddy without any trailer lights and walks up to talk with him. Needless to say, he does not have any of the paper work for a boat that does not even belong to him. In fact, the license plates on the trailer are expired. The trooper goes back to the patrol car to check things out, and he radios the post for a check on the registration plates for the trailer.

Now, the fun really begins!! Here sits our reluctant boat hauler stopped by the state troopers hauling a boat he has no idea who owns in the middle of the night. But! He is about to find out.

Into the post comes a call from the troopers asking for a check on a license plate. There seems to be something strange going on here! What in the world is our reluctant boat hauler doing running around in the middle of the night hauling a boat that belongs to the post commander! When this happens, bells go off and people start checking things out. They try to get hold of the post commander at home, but his phone is busy, so they end up getting hold of the city police to run by his house. The city police are at the door trying to contact the post commander who is on the phone with a long distance call and cannot make it to the door. Finally he gets to the door, and the city police ask him if his boat should be traveling down US-2 in the middle of the night. Of course not. His boat is in storage out at the local dealership for the winter! Wanna bet!!

Now, here sits our reluctant boat hauler, his day having gone from bad to worse, and his night surely not seeming to be getting any better at the moment. I can just hear him now, "But, officer, you are not going to believe this one....!"

There is an old "Yooper" proverb, " You hire cheap help, and you usually get just what you paid for!"

From The Land Where
The "Big"
Fish Live

Stories from
A Game Warden
by Sgt. John A. Walker

Sgt. Walker's third book

Chapter-11
Lucky Me? (3)

Wifee, I Really Do Love You

Well, 31 years ago today, I gave up my penthouse, Corvette sitting out in the carport, big screen TV, and all the other toys a single guy would have had during the time I had a wifee and four kids.

It would not have been that bad if my four kids had stayed away from all their mother's bad habits. Isn't it funny, but when they are good and do what's right, I sure can see Dad's qualities in them. But, when they make one of those "I can believe you did that" moves, it sure has to come from Mom's side of the family. I think most guys believe this is true.

The only other thing that I have come to understand after 31 years with wifee, and two grown girls, is that I could still have that new boat sitting out in the carport IF it wasn't for pantyhose!! Did you ever stop and think how many millions, or it could be even zillions, of dollars that the average dad spends on these crazy things? Just so they can hang all over the bathroom and get in his way all the time? Then the crazy ones I end up buying start out with a Walker in them, but it never fails that soon after they have a runnner in them and are useless!!! Unless I want to use them to varnish something.

I could never understand how they can make so many things that have such rough use out of the same material and it last, (Nylon football outfits, baseball uniforms, etc.) but these crazy things that ladies wear are useless. Really, I think it is all just another way of keeping us guys from having that little extra money in our pockets for important things, like a new gun or some fishing gear.

The suggestion of the week: If you have three ladies in your home wearing these crazy things at one time, make them a deal. Every time they need another pair, they have to place the same amount into a coffee can for the men in the family to have in a slush fund for their man-type important activities.

Or else I always thought I could go into the business of mass producing fish spawn bags for trout and salmon fishermen. It would make good use of all the panty hose that now have runners in them, plus just maybe I could recover some of the dollars lost to this investment each year.

But then you get thinking, you already have the zillions of panty hose laying around, but you would have to collect the fish spawn from the trout and salmon for your spawn bag tying business. Then to keep the fresh fish spawn fresh, both before and after you tied the spawn bags, you would have to invest in some refrigerators. Plus, you would have that fishy smell all over the house all the time. So to stop this, you would have to invest in a pole barn for your fish spawn bag tying business.

Just maybe it is cheaper to just keep buying the panty hose, living without your new boat and motor, and still figure you came out ahead.

O'well it sure has been a great time the last 31 years, **and** I really do not have much to complain about. After all, if any lady can put up living with a Yooper Game Warden, plus a guy that loves to hunt and be outdoors all the time, and his hunting dog, he had better be good to her and realize what he has.

Honey, I really do love you, the gray headed old grandpa of your dreams!!

Chapter-11
Lucky Me? (4)

You Would Think
An Old Game Warden Would Learn

A number of years ago while working with an "Old Game Warden", he gave me some fatherly advice. He said, " If you ever buy a gun you like, never get rid of it. Someone will offer you a couple of bucks for it, you'll sell it, then you'll blow the money on something and not even remember what it was. Then later on, you'll miss the gun you had and be sorry you ever sold it."

I listened to him and have never sold a gun once I bought one.

Back when my boys were still living at home, I made it a practice to bribe them to bring home a good report card by offering them a gun if they did. During high school they both ended up with a deer rifle, a muzzle loader, a 22-rifle, and a couple shotguns. It was money well spent, and I always told people, "It is still a lot cheaper than having to hire a lawyer to get them out of some trouble they may have got into."

This is one of those, "I'll never learn" stories.

Man! Not Again!

The other night I was talking to someone about living up here in Yooper land. We got to talking about the best place to eat in the area in years past. You know how gray headed old people are, they always talk about yesteryear.

I told them one of the worst places for me to eat was out at Garden Corners when I first moved here. Back then, Dean and Jacquie Head had a little place out there. It was not that the food was bad or the service was poor, it was the prices, they almost put me in the poor house! It seemed that whenever I took the wifee out there to eat, Dean had a great deal I just could not afford to pass up. You see, Dean was a gun dealer on the side. Only in Yooper land could a man take his wifee out for supper and it end up costing him over $200 for the meal, and the gun he brought home with him, or the scope, or the black powder and supplies.

You would think after a while even a "Yooper" would wise up and not get talked into it again, and again, and again.

The worst meal I ever had out there was just before Christmas one time. The chicken was great, I always had the same thing for supper, but one of Mr. Head's spies (his boy, Tim) had informed his dad that I just might be looking for something special for my boys for Christmas.

So here I come, with the wifee and kids, planning to spend under $20 for supper and returning home with a sane peace of mind, rather than returning home counting the days till next payday wondering if we could make it.

As I sat there enjoying my meal, Mr. Head walked over and said, I can hear it plain as day in my mind, "I hear you are looking for a couple of muzzle loaders for Christmas." My boys weren't there, and I could feel this almost fatal pain in the lower left hand side of my body, where my soon to be empty wallet lived. I wondered if I could pretend I was choking on a chicken bone, but with the luck I felt right now, it could really happen.

So, after I finished eating, I went over to the counter, and Mr. Head showed me these two muzzle loaders he just happened to have laying around. (Waiting for a sucker to stop by for supper!) They were really nice, both Thompson's 45 caliber, a couple of beautiful guns. But, I told Mr. Head there was no way I could afford them as bad as I would like to have them.

A little while later, as I drove home with the wifee and the kids, also two Thompson muzzle loaders with all the extras, I wondered how a Yooper with half a brain could ever go out for a nice quiet supper in the middle nowhere, and end up spending $520 for a night out with the wifee!!

Also, knowing the heart burn he now felt was not caused by the chicken dinner.

Chapter-12

Kids Please Listen

The Empty Rocking Chair

Kids, I sit here before my new computer and think of just how things have changed since I was a youth. Just stop with me and think back a minute: There were no jet planes, there were no TVs in our town, the telephone went through an operator, the police were contacted by a police light on the front of the bank that was turned on when a call came in, and most kids I grew up with had never been out of the U.P.

Still, I had something back then that so many youth are missing out on today. I had a mom and dad that loved me. They were there, together, all the time I was growing up. Now I am over a half century old, and if there is one thing I miss, it's not having my dad around when it comes time to make a major decision.

I can recall just like it was yesterday sitting out at hunting camp as my dad sat in his rocking chair before the fire and talking to him as two buddies would sit and talk. You could always ask my dad for advice, and you never felt that he was a "know-it-all" trying to tell you what to do. He was just a friend you could call on when you needed one. He was always in your corner and wanted the best for you.

It has been almost thirty years ago now since my dad passed away, while on vacation down at my house in lower Michigan. It has meant almost thirty deer seasons where they are just not the same when dad is not around anymore to make them special. It means a good number of grandkids that never even got to meet Grandpa and have him be that special kind of person in their young lives.

Now, you would have needed a dad like I did to understand what I am trying to say. Without any formal education to speak of, he was a first class husband and father. It was something books did not teach, unless it was **"The Book"**. My Dad was not a well traveled man in the eyes of the world, but he had more wisdom than many a person that was. (Some of whom I have met in my travels.) Dad knew how to take part in all that his kids did; he knew what was important to us. He knew how to make each and every one of us feel like we were something special. Dad knew how to make special days something important, even when there was not much money to be spent on doing it. Let me point a few things out to you from the heart of this old man.

First let me say, as I talk about these things, that my mom and dad were a team. I may point out things that Dad and I did, but Mom was always there, too. If you have read my other books you are aware of this.

When we were growing up, our birthdays were something special. It meant a birthday cake all your own, and Dad's rule was you always had a cake no matter how hard times may be. I can remember my mom hoarding and saving eggs trying to get enough set aside to bake an Angel Food cake (even though Dad always hinted that a Devil's Food cake might fit the bill better.) But, the cake was always there. In fact when my mom passed away, there were dozens of Angel Food cake mixes (now they come in a box, they never used to) in her cupboard. She used to make them for people, even grown up people, that had never had anyone bake them a birthday cake, just to show them there was someone who cared about them.

The other thing on your birthday was a rule direct from Dad that you did not have to help with the dishes or any other chores around the house. It was **your** day. It was a special day, and maybe my parents did not have money to spend, but they could still make it your special day.

Kids, there was another rule. You **always** did your schoolwork! And if you ever got into trouble at school, you had better hope and pray that Dad never found out about it! My dad may have never finished school, but he soon learned how important it was that his kids did. Both Mom and Dad always took a **personal** interest in how and what we did at school. My dad was never a basketball nut, but when his boy was on the team, if Dad was not working, he never missed a game. I still wonder if he knew or really cared what basketball was all about or what was going on. It didn't matter. His boy was on the team, on the bench, across the gym from him, watching the game being played the same as Dad was. That didn't matter either. His boy was involved, so he was there.

I can sit here almost forty years later and remember this incident like it was yesterday. My brothers and myself were out hunting with Dad one afternoon. It was one of those days when we could all get together and spend some of that special time hunting. On this day Dad had to leave early in the afternoon to head back for town so he could attend a union meeting. At the time he was one of the officials in the union at the papermill. To Dad, this was a real important job that he held in the union. His dad had held one before him, and he had followed in his dad's footsteps. On this day, I can recall Dad talking like he was standing by my side today saying, "Well boys, I guess it's time for Dad to give up his union job. When it comes between me and my family doing things together, it's time to give it up." And he did. I guess I never realized till years later the true sacrifice he made for us, but it sure let us know how important he thought we were.

 When the fall of the year rolled around and we got to spend our first overnight stay at camp for the year, the first night there, Dad would always take out the new hunting guide, give it to us, and tell us to read it and look for any changes in it. He had his own way of teaching us that rules and laws were important, and it was up to us to know them. I can still remember sitting there one night and asking Dad, "Dad, how come you quit shooting deer out of season?" (You have to remember that back during the "Big Depression" it was the normal thing to take deer up in this area for food, but I cannot ever remember my dad bringing an illegal deer home.) Dad looked at me and said, "Son, how in the world could I be out shooting illegal deer when all you kids know that it is wrong and at the same time be asking you kids to do right in school, obey the rules, and always, always do right, if I am not obeying the rules? It just wouldn't work." It was one of the best lessons I ever learned from my dad.

I can always remember my dad taking an interest in his kids' lives. I would sit at camp, and Dad would ask me how things were going in school and the conversation would get around to what lay ahead in life. Dad always encouraged us to set goals. "If you set a goal and come up a little short, you will still be a lot better off than if you never set one." As I have stated before, I had the job my dad always wanted to have. He loved the outdoors and the time we spent out there. Sometimes the turns in life do not always let you do everything you would like to do, but sometimes you can steer someone else in that direction and be so proud when they make it. My dad did this with us.

Kids, I cannot ever remember my dad coming right out and telling me in words, "I love you". But there was never any doubt in my mind that he did. He showed it by what he did, how he lived, and what he thought of us. I guess it is one of those times you could say that actions spoke louder than words. I can recall the time a few months after getting out of high school that my dad and mom took me over to Ironwood to catch an airplane to go into the service. My big, manly dad stood there with tears in his eyes, gave me a big bear hug, and I knew he loved me and always would be in my corner.

Now I sit, years and years later, and would give almost anything to be able to just sit before the fireplace at hunting camp, to just spend some time with my dad. Just to talk with him man to man. But it can never be. So kids, take the time to be with Dad. He is the best buddy you will ever have. Kids, take my word for it, you may have a lot of friends as you go through life, **but,** there is always only one dad, the guy who can seem to read your heart and soul. I don't care how many mountains you climb and what you accomplish during life, it just will not be the same when you can no longer call your dad just to say, "Dad, guess what happened to me today......" For all of us comes that day that the old rocking chair at hunting camp sits empty, and Dad is no longer there to spend time with. Just to enjoy because he's dad.... Make the most of today, and make every day that you get to spend with him a special day, because they are and should be.

P.S. Dads: In my travels peddling my books, I have been told that today in our country the average dad spends just thirty-seven (37) seconds in personal time with each one of his children per day. Even if it should be thirty-seven minutes per day, is it any wonder our nation is in the shape it is?

Chapter-13
Youth

As you travel around as a Game Warden, you get to hear and see just about everything. If moms ever realized all that happened out in the woods as their boys were having "fun", they would never let them out of the house ever again. These are a few short tales of youth having fun.

A Running Start

On this evening during the firearm deer season, I was working with another officer who had located a number of illegal scaffolds being used to hunt from. (In Michigan it is against the law to hunt from a tree with a firearm.)

We were patrolling an area of the Garden Peninsula. The scaffold we were going to check was next to a pine plantation. It was up in a big, old birch tree a good ways off the ground. Our plan was to come around the plantation on a two-track till we could hide the car and walk up to the scaffold on foot. Things were going pretty well as we came into the area and started around the plantation.

As we got almost to the area where we planned on hiding the patrol car and walking , I could hear the other officer yell, "There he goes!" He was out of the car that quick and off running through the trees. (It seemed that the scaffold was a couple of rows closer to the two-track than we thought it was.)

I pulled up to the birch tree that held the scaffold and parked there to wait for my partner. A little while later he came back with the young lad in tow who had taken off running when he first saw us.

There was only one problem!

It seems that in some areas you learn quick to just start running when you first see a Game Warden's car, then later stop and figure out why you ran. This is what the party did.

The only problem was when he started running he was twenty feet up in a tree standing on a scaffold! I ask him what he thought of that first step. He told me, "Man! It was a lot farther down than I thought it was before I took that first step!"

One in the Freezer

There is nothing like first coming of age and being able to go out hunting, instead of just tagging along behind dad. When this happens, there is only once in life that you get the chance to take your first shot at something. It is a time you will never forget, even if you try to.

When you stop and think of it, there is nothing like a Dad and his son when they first get out hunting together. This is one of those cases.

The boy and his dad had made plans so after school they had a place on their property where the lad could sit up in a tree blind watching for deer. It was a good spot, and the boy saw a lot of deer, and even had some pretty good shots if he wanted to take a doe, but he had his heart set on a buck for his first deer.

On this evening this boy was up in his tree stand still trying for his first deer with his bow and arrows. He knew what he had to do, sit quiet, don't fall asleep, wait for a good clean shot, ... On this evening just when things should start happening, he spotted some movement! As he watched and could now tell it was a deer, out stepped a nice buck and moved towards the area of his stand. Not really a trophy buck, but isn't the first one always a trophy? A nice four point, just what he had been waiting for.

He watched and waited. Things had to be just right, waiting like he was taught, it would work out. Then the moment came, the buck was standing at the right angle, the distance for a good shot was within range, and things were looking great. Our lad slowly pulled back on his bow, real slow and steady, not too much movement, wait till you calm down a little and your heart stops pounding through your shirt, wait just the right moment, calm, cool, everything smooth, **now!!**

But just a minute!! Out of the corner of his eye he sees some movement! He turns his head just a little so he can see what it is, and out steps a **really** nice eight point buck! A real trophy for a first timer or anyone else! Just maybe he can get the big one, just maybe...

Now our lad has a four point right in front of him and a big eight point coming in! Our young hunter, as all us hunters have done if we are truthful, starts shaking so bad, and it feels like his heart is going to jump right out of his chest, his lungs are not working right anymore and he cannot get his breath, his nerves are now shot. Now he is shaking so badly his arrow vibrates off the nock on the bow and falls down to the ground! The noise of the arrow falling through the branches onto the ground scares off both bucks, both the little four point and the monster eight point.

Lesson learned: A four point in the freezer is bigger and better then an eight point still on the hoof!!

OK Mom, When You Put It That Way

If you have read the other three books I have written, you know that I married a sweet little gal out of the hills of Missouri. My wifee is 100% a lady, but this doesn't mean she cannot hit a baseball, shoot a basketball, and fire a gun. I met my wifee when we flew out of Arizona on maneuvers into the Ozarks. We were running a test to see if you could drop equipment from airplanes into openings in the mountains. We were told that the terrain was something like the hills in Vietnam, and they were testing to see what could survive the impact with the ground. Take my word for it, not much did.

But back to wifee. I met her down in Mountain Grove, Mo. when she lived in town so she could work at a local factory. It was a while before I got to go back into the hills to meet her family. The first time I went back to the farm, a number of her brothers were home on this Sunday afternoon. They were out at the edge of a field next to the house shooting a 308 rifle at a target across the field. One of the boys asked me if I wanted to take a shot.

Here I was with a rifle I had never fired before in my life, shooting at a coffee can filled with water across a forty acre field. What could I say? I always figured this was the big test. If I hit the can I got a wife, if I missed the can it meant I was still looking. I picked up the rifle, laid down on the ground and took aim. I squeezed the trigger and hit the coffee can and got a wife.

Years later on a weekend afternoon we had been out to some friends' house in Cooks. On the way home, we stopped off at a sand pit to do some target shooting with my pistol. Here I was with two teenage boys shooting at cans. The boys both could shoot pretty well, but they were still young enough they missed more cans than they hit. But we were having fun as a dad and his boys will out in the woods as Mom sat and watched.

After we had shot for a while and were about ready to leave, I asked their Mom if she would like to take a couple of shots. She got out of the pickup while I set out a couple of cans and reloaded my 357. Little, lady-like Mom took the pistol from me, stepped to the edge of the sand pit, and took aim as her two boys watched.

Bang! Plunk!, Bang! Plunk!, Bang! Plunk!, was the way it went till the gun was empty and all the cans went flying! Could you believe it! Mom! I'm not sure her two sons could, but I could because I had been around her enough to know her better.

We picked up the cans, put the pistols away, and headed home without too much talk from her sons who were still wondering, "Who is this gal that can shoot like that?!" But what a way to impress your boys and earn a little backwoods respect.

I always figured if I had any trouble with my boys as they were growing up, which I never did, I would just have wifee strap on a pistol to get their attention and the problems would be solved.

Last hunt with Dad

Dad's spot at camp

Now the empty rocking chair

Grandma's Laces

A keeper?

I saw you first!!!

The end of a great day with my dog and buddies

The best of times

Illegal Fish

The symbol of our town, Manistique

Both a sure sign of our freedom

Replica of Vietnam Wall at Marquette

Chapter-14

I Really Shouldn't Tell You This, But.....

For the last part of my career, I worked in the area of the U.P. that included part of the Garden Peninsula. This area for years was talked about in newspapers and articles on account of some of the problems down there.

There were some problems with a few outlaws, but you have to remember that as tales are told and retold, they sometimes get more interesting with each telling. This is the case with some of the tales from the Garden Peninsula. But, it sure made for some interesting times when a new recruit would come up to work this area with me. They may have been big and tough down in the asphalt jungle, but they walked a different walk while patrolling the Peninsula.

Welcome Aboard

On this morning I was on patrol with a brand new officer who had just come up from the Saginaw area to work with me. It was just before the start of bear season, and we were patrolling looking for bear blinds and any activity from early bear hunters. In our travels, we headed down Little Harbor Road onto the famous Garden Peninsula. As we drove along I was asked question after question about what the area was like and what to expect.

Now it was not that he was scared of the work, he had just heard so many stories he did not know what to expect. Of course, you know me, I wouldn't add any fuel to the fire as I told him about working up in the land where a Game Warden is really a Game Warden.

A short while later we cut off Little Harbor Road to the west and hit some 2-track trails. We were traveling along a creek when we saw A foot path through the ferns. We got out and checked these out and figured they may be someone traveling back and forth to bait a bear blind.

I told the new officer that I would walk the foot path and he could take the pickup back down the 2-track so I could meet him when I came out of the woods.

Now understand, all morning we had been talking about all the stories about working the Garden Peninsula. This officer was new to the area, and now he was down onto the Peninsula almost too close to Garden itself. But he never said a word, just looked at me, got into the truck all by himself, and headed down the 2-track. I started walking back into the woods along the foot-path through the shoulder high ferns.

It was not long before I realized that the trail I was following was not bear hunters, but it was someone who had walked into the creek and then followed it back towards the road. Seeing I was already in to the creek and the pickup had gone, I figured I may as well just follow the creek and the path back towards the road. Just a little ways from the road, the path came back out right next to the 2-track. I glanced down the 2-track and saw the pickup coming slowly towards me. The foot-path had allowed me to get ahead of him seeing I had a shorter distance to travel.

All of a sudden that little guy that will get you in trouble now and then came to life. Here comes this new to Yooper Land officer, in the middle of nowhere, wondering who and what he might meet on the famous Garden Peninsula. Here crouched down in the high ferns lays this old officer from the "What goes around, comes around" school. And he gets thinking and waiting, still unobserved.

As the pickup putted along the 2-track closer and closer, I waited till it was right next to me now only a couple of feet away, and me laying in the ferns. I took out my pistol, pointed it at the ground, and fired three times as fast as I could pull the trigger!!!

You know it is amazing how fast the human body can bounce between the seat and the roof of a pickup truck before it settles down after being sacred out of its wits.

(I know how it feels, I have been there a number of times, on the other end, out in the middle of nowhere when someone decided to scare the fire out of me.)

Fishermen Are Nuts!

After spending so much time in the woods and on the water checking fishermen I think I have found enough facts to prove this theory. In fact, I am sure that most people tend to, or are at least supposed to, get wiser as they get older. Not true with fishermen.

This could fall under having a real bad "Yooper" day.

It seems there were a couple of guys that went out fishing. They headed back to that famous place called "the middle of nowhere". Nobody to bother you, nobody to help you, no AAA, just you, your buddy, and the world.

They got where they had to stop and park their pickup, grabbed their fishing gear, and off they went through the woods for a great time on a trout stream. Things went pretty good, but I never did hear if they caught anything.

Now, the key to this story is that one of the party was just transplanted to our famous U.P. from "city" life down south. In other words, a "City dude" who had married his guide's daughter. Dad was out to teach him the "Yooper" way of doing things.

After they got done fishing, they walked back to their pickup truck, threw their fishing gear into the back, and went to get into the cab of the pickup to return home ump-teen miles away. You will notice I said, **"and went to get into their pickup truck"**. Because, both doors were locked! **No Problem!** "City dudes" always lock doors even up here where people never do. But, the keys for the pickup were where they always were, maybe rusted in, still in the ignition!! I mean they both knew this, they could see them, hanging in the ignition, so close, yet so far away. I mean all you had to do was look through the window, and there they were, swinging back and forth.....No calling AAA, no coat hangers hanging around, nothing.

It seems that you had a break down in cultures here. The older, "Yooper" for longer, knew that in the U.P. you never remove keys from your vehicle's ignition! You could lose them! Then where would you be? Out in the middle of no-where without any keys. On top of this, you never, never lock up a vehicle in the U.P.! Because number one, you always leave your keys in the ignition so you know where they are, and number two, why spend half your life locking and unlocking doors when you know good and well that you are the only one who even "knows" about this secret fishing place!!

But, "city-dude" was bought up in the world where if you are going to be out of sight of your vehicle, you always lock it up! So here they stood.....Son-in-law not really wanting to say too much, because they were miles and miles from AAA or any help. But thank goodness his father-in-law had another key! **A "Yooper"" type key!** He reaches down, grabs this big rock, and knocks out one of the side windows of the pickup!! Then reaching in, unlocks the door, yells to the still shocked city-dude-son-in-law, "Get in! We have to get moving."

As the son-in-law looks at the glass laying all over the seat, he wonders if he will live to get home or be cut to shreds before they make it.

Only A Dad...

Did you ever wonder how kids put up with dads? In my travels I have to wonder at times. It had to be a full time project just training dads to do things right.

This story took place with one of the teenagers from our youth group.

This boy had finally reached that long awaited for fourteenth birthday!! This means you now can make your first real, I can now hunt, trip with Dad to deer camp. This boy was all set, ready or not.

Now remember when you have Dad plus a number of others in the family, deer rifles can be hard to come by. Put on top of this the fact it is usually first come, first gets one. So as in so many cases, you get what's left. But who cares. You are now an official deer hunter old enough to shoot a buck on your own, almost.

Our lad gets everything ready, and they all spend the night before season out at camp. First thing opening morning, off they go, each one to his own deer blind. Well, I really do not know how to tell the rest of the story....

But, there is this dad from the town that I live in that sent his "new-to hunting" son out to hunt deer with a deer rifle that could not hit anything!!!

This is this boy's first year hunting, and I guess his dad does not want him to get a big head. So here he sits in his deer blind, waiting for that buck to come in, with the last of the inventory of family rifles, with the rifle's stock that is not firmly attached to the action of the rifle!!

Now this would work just great if you were sitting in your deer blind and a deer came sneaking up from off to one side or the other. You could shoot at a deer in any direction without ever having to move your body! All you would do is, just hold the stock firmly against your shoulder, then move the barrel and action slowly in the direction of the deer, while all the time you are still facing forward.

Boy! Can't you just see the surprised look on the deer's face when this hunter is looking one way and shooting at it in another direction? In fact, it will really surprise the deer if you even hit it! It sure is amazing what some kids have to put up with, but I guess dads will always be dads.

In fact I felt so sorry for the boy I gave him one of my deer rifles to use. Wouldn't you know it, he got one and I got skunked!

I Think Maybe We're Stuck!

There is one thing for certain if you are out working the field as a game warden, that is the fact that you are always looking for a good place to hide. It has to be the type place where you can sneak in and out without anybody knowing you are even in the area. It also has to be the type place where you are out of sight when a vehicle may go by shining, or someone may want to check and see if the game warden is in the area. It is a never-ending project trying to find the perfect place.

One of the best places I had downstate to use during fish runs was a house that was under construction. This was a ranch style house with an attached garage. The house was roughed in pretty well when the fish runs started, so I would just back into the garage. There was no door on the garage at this time in the construction, so it worked perfectly as a place to sit and watch the cuts for pike spearers.

Another place I had was in a field where they had stored a large number of these large round bales of hay. When we were checking things out, we found an opening that was just large enough to back the patrol unit between the bales and hide it. It worked pretty well till the snow and wet weather came.

Here are a few hiding place tales:

It seems that there was this old farmhouse that had been empty for years. There was the house, a barn, and an old garage sitting together. The house sat a good distance off the gravel road out in front of it, and between the house and the road were a couple of dozen old apple trees. If an officer took his patrol unit up the drive, then backed between the house and the garage, he could get behind the house with a perfect place to hide. The house sat on a little hill, on a curve, so you could see cars coming and going both ways. It was perfect, and nobody was ever around the house itself.

In order to get into the area to hide, the officers usually would come the last couple of miles up the road without lights, running just in the moon light. They had been hiding here so long, they could do this, pull into the driveway, and back behind the house really without looking or seeing where they were going.

On this night two officers were working together and decided to sit in the area of the old house for awhile. I would hate to guess how many good shining cases were made from this spot through the years. The officers did what was always done. When about two miles from the old house, they killed their headlights and drove down the road to the orchard in front of the house. They then turned around and backed between the house and the garage to the area behind the house. **All of a sudden,** they fell off the edge of the world. The car dropped down in the back, the bumper crashed into something, bounced off it, and the front end came down with another crash. After the effects of whip-lash wore off, the officers turned on their headlights.

Here they sat with a wall of dirt all the way around them. There was about six or seven feet of dirt out each window, straight up and down. As they looked around, they found that some inconsiderate person had come into the area of the house since the last time they had hid there and dug a basement hole for a new house!! Could you believe it!

This is not the worst part of the story, because now they had to do what every officer hates to do. They had to get on the radio and call out for help. Take my word for it, it is hard to drive a car out of a basement. In the good old days, one of the best tools we had to catch violators was the airplane. When you stop and think about all the area each officer has to cover, there is no way you could ever cover it by yourself. So to do a better job, there were officers that were pilots, and the department owned a number of planes.

Voices In The Dark

When activity was at its highest, we would set up group patrols to cover as much area as we could with the few officers we had using the airplane. (I could write a whole chapter on some of our pilots alone, but it is enough to say that most of them are nuts for what they do.) On this night we had assigned officers to certain areas to be ready if the plane spotted any shiners.

One of the officers was sitting in the area of a number of old abandoned farms. In this area were a lot of old apple trees that still produced some apples. There were also a lot of deer that came into these openings after dark.

The major problem we usually ran into while working with the airplane was the weather. It could be nice on the ground, and the plane up in the air could be icing up. Or with the strange U.P. weather, we could have the type weather that produced a lot of ground fog. This is the type fog that hangs right near the ground and keeps the airplane from observing things on the ground.

On this evening the officer that was sitting near the old orchard all of a sudden was surrounded by ground fog. He could not see a thing. Then he heard a vehicle moving around somewhere in the fog. Heard it stop, a shot was fired, and they heard a door open. The violators were that close, and it was that quiet, and sound was really carrying that night.

The officers then heard some people talking. In fact, they heard one of the subjects count the points on the buck they had just shot. But, with the fog having moved in so heavily, they could not find the violators or their vehicle. They heard the deer thrown into the back of a vehicle and

then the violators took off going somewhere in the fog. The officers
called for the airplane to help them, and we headed over into their area.
Believe it or not, even after being close enough to hear the outlaws talking, they were never located. Two cars and an airplane working the area
could not see enough through the fog to find them.

No! It Couldn't Be!!

One night I was on patrol with another officer during the firearm deer
season. We were way up north in the National Forest running without
lights along a gravel road. Things had been rather slow, and we were
just putting along talking to each other.

All of a sudden we saw the glow of headlights coming our way. The
approaching vehicle was still a couple of curves away, so we pulled into
a two track trail, stopped and let it go by. We then fell in behind this
vehicle to follow it for awhile. We were still traveling without any lights
on, and it was well after midnight.

After a ways, the vehicle we were following turned to the right down
one of those U.S. Forest Service roads leading to the middle-of-no-
where, then dead ending. We thought just maybe this crew might be up
to something. After we had covered a couple of miles, we saw the vehicle stop, so we backed up putting a couple of curves between us and the
car we had been following. We then got out and stood by the patrol car
and waited to see what they were up to.

It was not long before we were to realize that this crew had just
returned to camp. We could hear them really cutting up with each other,
yelling and screaming in their horse play. They just had to be a crew of
"Trolls" up in the middle-of-no-where, just enjoying God's great north
woods figuring there was nobody for miles around. We listened for
awhile, then got ready to leave. Still we had not used any lights, and
these "Trolls" had no idea there was another living soul anywhere
around.

I figured, let's have some fun and see what happens. So I reached down
and turned up the P.A. system on the patrol car as loud as it would go
and yelled, **"This is the Lord talking! Hold it down out here! Don't
you realize all my little animals are trying to get a good night's
sleep! Now just quiet down and go to bed right now!!"**

Man, this crew of five or six men went from yelling and carrying on to dead silence as if someone turned off a switch on their voice box. I mean all of a sudden there was not a sound at all out in the woods but two game wardens trying their best to keep from breaking out laughing. We stood by the car for ten, fifteen minutes longer before we got in to leave, and still there was not another sound from the hunting camp around the curve.

I have often wondered what story this crew told after they returned home, "Honey, I know they always called the U.P. God's country but................."

A 95 Miles An Hour Bear!

I don't care where you work or what part of the country you live in, there is always someone living in the area that has a problem. I mean, there is always this guy that took a curve too fast one time in life, and a few of his bricks flew off the top of his load. There is usually nothing you can do about these people but just shrug your shoulders and learn to live with it.

In one of the areas where I worked, there was this type person. Thank goodness he liked to call the county sheriff department with his problem and did not have the local game warden's number. But, the deputies were always trying to give me his problem simply because it seemed to be more in my field.

It seems this guy had a real problem upstairs, in more ways than one. Next to his house was a tree. Now, according to our complaintant there was this large black bear that would climb up this tree next to his house, open his upstairs bedroom window, crawl into his house, then go running through his bedroom, down the stairs and off out the front door back to the woods! I mean to tell you, this guy was serious about this bear problem.

He would call the sheriff department at all hours of the day and night wanting them to do something about his imaginary bear. "Trap it! Shoot it! Just get rid of it!"
Personally, I really got a kick out of this, mainly because it wasn't me that had to answer all this guy's calls.

One night I was out on patrol riding with one of the county deputies. We were patroling the southern part of the county when we received a complaint that took us towards the east. It was right around midnight when the call came in and we took off to head over to contact the people. As we approached the little town where our party with the bear problem lived, we saw his house on the south side of the road about a mile in front of us.

As we looked we could see that all lights were on in the house. We then observed our deputy's favorite buddy standing out in the yard with the yard light on and holding a flashlight. The deputy said, "O'no, here we go again. You watch, we will be getting a phone call about his bear problem again."

I said, "I'll fix that." I reached down on the transmission hump and turned on the overhead P.A. system as loud as it would go. I then grabbed the mike as we went flying by this guy standing out in his yard with a flashlight at about ninety-five miles an hour. As we went by I yelled into the mike as loud as I could, "Greeeeeeeeeareeeeeeeeeeee!!!" And we were gone off into the dark. The deputy about died, figuring he would get into hot water over it "if" the party had turned around fast enough to see the patrol car.

Early the next morning I stopped by the sheriff department for coffee. A group of us were sitting in the coffee room, right off the main lobby, still laughing about the night before, when in walked our party with the bear problem right up to the lobby desk. As a few of us were trying to figure out how to fast fade into the sunrise, he walked up to the deputy sitting behind the desk and said, "I'm moving, I'm moving! Last night I not only saw that bear again, but I also heard him growl at me as he went flying by the front of my house!! I'm moving!" He turned around and walked out the door.

And he did. He left the county, and the bear must have followed him because there was never another complaint about it.

Chapter-15
I Hate Trailers!

Before you even get into these couple of short stories, I have to explain a few things about living in the "Frozen Chosen U.P.". Now if there is one never ending project, it's working on trailers. With the snow and all the salt they put on the roads, there is always something going wrong. If you ever hooked up a trailer after a couple of winters use, and all the lights worked on it at one time, you would figure you had died and gone to heaven. There is no doubt in my mind that there is a conspiracy to make wiring for trailers so it just won't last. But enough said, into some tales about trailers.

I Wonder Where My Trailer Went?
(You can sing this if you feel led)

Back in the "good old days" when I first started as a game warden, there were no snowmobiles to use. Later on, for a number of years, if an officer used a snowmobile it was his own, his own gas, and he paid for his own upkeep. **But!** Then the state finally bought some snowmachines for us to use. The new machines were **8-horsepower** Polaris, and believe it or not, we thought they were the perfect improvement. Now look around and see what the new generation is griping about having!

There was only one slight problem! Whoever over in the *Big House* decided to purchase us this new piece of equipment must have run it through those guys sitting in front of a computer, with glasses that are at least 1/2 inch thick, who ride a bicycle back and forth to work each day, and never were outside the asphalt jungle in their lives! Here we were with our brand new snowmachines ready to go to work out on the ice of Saginaw Bay to check ice fishermen, but we only had one little problem! There were no trailers with which to move the new snowmachines from place to place.

Then someone else got a *really good* idea? Out behind most, then Conservation Department buildings, were old boat trailers they had junked right after the Civil War. So why not use these for snowmobile trailers? They just took a piece of plywood and bolted it to the frame of the old boat trailers to make a flat bed to place the snowmobiles on. There was a saying back then, "What you have now is better than nothing at all." But I was soon to find out that this saying may not be true.

Off I went heading out with my new snowmobile, to check out a few places where I could not get to before. During the course of my travels, I took River Road that wound through the woods following the snaky course of the river that ran through the county. Happy as a lark was this officer without a care in the world, that is, till I happened to glance in my rearview mirror!!

I glanced, then looked again. It couldn't be, but it is. There is no longer any snowmobile following along behind my patrol car!! I stopped the car as quickly as I could, jumped out, and ran to the back of the car and looked! Sure enough, the snowmobile and trailer were gone, but still firmly attached to the ball on the trailer hitch was the tongue of the trailer! Now my biggest fear happened to come to mind.

If the trailer came unhooked while rounding a curve one way, great, because this means my snowmobile is just sitting behind me out in the ditch or at worst in the woods somewhere. **But!** If my new snowmobile with its remarkable trailer came off while rounding a curve the other way, my new snowmobile is no longer a snowmobile, but maybe a boat out in the middle of the river.

I turned around and headed back up the road looking for what might be left of my snowmobile. As luck would have it, it came off on the right turn in the road, so it just went off the road into the ditch and stopped.

After this happened I went to plan **B**. The state may have finally bought me a snowmobile so that I no longer had to use my own, but till they broke down and bought a trailer to haul it around on, I would use my own!

I Hate It When That Happens

This is another tale of a make-your-own-trailer adventure. To go on camping trips and to take the family on vacation, I made up this ideal trailer to use. I bought an old single snowmobile trailer and built a plywood box on it. This thing was large enough to hold anything and everything you could want to take along. In fact, besides what you could put in the trailer, I had built a bike rack on top and on the front of the trailer so we could take these too. It was a jewel of fine workmanship.

On this trip we were going down to Missouri to see the wifee's family. We had the four kids at home then, so we took enough junk to cover all occasions no matter what we might want to do. At this time I owned a Chevy pickup with an overhead camper. We had set this up with an intercom so the kids could ride in the back with Mom and I up front. It worked great.

Off we headed for the thousand mile trip down to see Grandpa. Back in those days, I always liked to leave after work and travel at night. The kids would go to sleep, and there was less traffic. I soon learned that after dark I could see the reflection of the trailer lights in the big outside mirrors on the pickup. Also, if I hit the brake lights, I could see the reflection of all the bicycles on top of the trailer. What the life! I had the world by the tail and everything a guy could want in life. I had finally figured out how to travel with a crew of kids. Buy a camper, put them in it, then build a trailer and bring along everything you own.

Things were going great. About three hundred and fifty miles from home we were traveling through the Chicago area making good time without a care in the world. That is, until we were traveling on the six lane, and I made the mistake of looking in my outside, driver's side, rearview mirror!! As I glanced into the mirror, I noticed this strange looking vehicle pull out from behind my trailer into the next lane and go to pass me. I looked, then looked again! It was not another vehicle, although it may depend on how you look at it, **it was my trailer that had pulled out to pass my pickup!**

I may be a "Yooper", and I may be from the backwoods, but I know trailers are supposed to be followers, not leaders in this world. So just to show it who was boss, I sped up, pulled over into it's lane and slowed. The trailer still wanted to get to the front of the line, so it ran into the back of my truck, but I just slowly slowed down and worked my way over to the side of the expressway and stopped.

After getting out and checking, I found that the trailer had somehow jumped off the ball on the trailer hitch. I hooked it back up, took about ninety miles of baling wire (A "Yooper's" way of fixing anything and everything before duct tape came along.) and made sure it would never come off again. And it didn't.

Smarter?

As you can see by the two tales above, I have real luck with home-made trailers. So there is only one thing a guy can do as he gets older and wiser. I went out and bought me a new, factory made, two wheel trailer to haul all my junk in. One of my goals in life is for the day to come where I can travel without having to take everything we do now. Therefore, there will be no need to haul a trailer along behind.

I have not yet arrived.

In the "year of 1996" I figured just maybe I had arrived, but I soon found out it was not to be. This time it was not my kids, yet maybe it was. At home now with Mommy and me, there is only my baby girl. All six foot of her. She is going to be eighteen this year. But, I figured with just the three of us to travel now, we could make it with just usens and what we could place in the trunk of the car, right? **Wrong!**

We had made plans to travel down to my other daughter's in Florida for Easter. I did not know that my daughter had made plans for a family-get-together. The one boy and his family were flying up from Texas to meet us. The other boy had business in Georgia, so we were to go through Madison, WI, pick up his wife and our two grandkids to take to Florida with us. Do you realize what this means? You guessed it! Pull the trailer out of the snow bank and hook it up. But, don't worry, remember this is a "store bought" trailer.

We made it to Madison, loaded up the whole crew, hi-chairs, cribs, at least 3,000 diapers, and off we went for the eleven hundred mile trip all the way to Florida and back. I bet you thought after reading the other two stories that something happened with the full car and trailer, in the middle-of-nowhere between Madison and Florida. Wrong.

We had a great time all the way down and back with the grandkids, daughter-in-law, wifee, and Cathy. After we got back to Madison, we dropped off the boy's family and all their gear. It was about 5:00 in the evening, so we made plans to drive the last three hundred miles home the same day.

We got about twenty miles from the boy's house traveling on a four-lane, when all of a sudden, the car shook like crazy. I glanced up in the rearview mirror and saw fire flying, and all the cars behind me on the expressway scattering like a flock of quail. I also noticed a little trailer wheel in the emergency lane coming up hard and fast on the inside!

I pulled over onto the grass and walked back to find my tire. (Do you have any idea how far a little trailer tire can travel on an expressway when it is not handicapped by the rest of the trailer and the car?) I finally found it. All this time I'm really just being thankful it happened when it did. It could have happened on our trip to Florida, hundreds of miles from anyone we knew. I unhooked the now one-wheel trailer, took everything out of it and placed it in the car. That is, everything but a real large Rubber Maid container too big to fit in the car. After twenty-five years in law enforcement, I know people.

We turned around and headed back to the boy's house. The boy and his helper were working and had a pickup with them, so we took the pickup back to load the trailer in so he could haul it back to his house. (This trailer, the three of us could pick up and put in the back of the truck.) As we approached the area where we had left the trailer, my daughter said, "Dad, it's funny that nobody even bothered to stop and see if we needed any help?" I told her it seems to be the way life is today.

As we came over a little hill where we could see our now wheel-less trailer, we saw that someone had indeed stopped to see what was going on with my trailer. (Could my daughter have been wrong in the fact nobody cared?) In fact, just as we were coming up to the trailer, the man, standing by the trailer with his wife, took my large Rubber Maid container out of the trailer and threw it into the back of his truck!

I sped up and pulled right across in front of the truck as they were jumping into the cab to take off, as my boy came flying up behind the truck in the pickup. **Surprise!!!!!** As I was getting out of the car, my Wifee was saying, "Now, John, John behave!" *Who me! Not behave? Never!*

I walked back to the driver's side of the pickup where the driver was now halfway back out of his truck. I kindly said or explained to him, "I think that object you just removed from that trailer may belong to me, seeing the trailer belongs to me?" The man was still standing there with his mouth hanging open trying to talk. But, his wife had no trouble talking and explaining to us that there was nobody around, so they didn't know!

One thought went through my mind. I had to wonder if it had been a boat trailer or a trailer full of hunting or camping gear that had a problem and lost a wheel, would they have cleaned this trailer out, too? If so, you could only hope and wish they would someday run into a judge like Judge Stark back in "Yooper Land" who feels that someone who will steal from another hunter or fisherman is deserving of whatever they may get.

Chapter-16
Christmas of the 90's?

I guess that one of the things that really gets to my wife and me is Christmas time in the 90's. After the way we both grew up, this time of year is really important and special to us.

In fact, there were only two times a year when a boy growing up when I did could expect to receive something special, just for him. It was first on your birthday and then at Christmas. But, it was almost always only one item that Mom and Dad had to save for and put a special effort into getting for you. I guess this is what made Christmas so special.

It now bothers both of us when we see so many homes where the Christmas tree has more gifts under it than the stores had back when we were young. What are we teaching our youth?

I have told this while talking to college classes, speaking to church groups, and senior citizen groups.

"There is not a thing in the world I want. I say this from the bottom of my heart. If you asked me to make a list of something I would like for a gift, what could I put on it? I already have everything a party could want. If my wife, children, and now grandchildren are healthy and serving the Lord with their lives, what more could a man ask for? I already have it all."

The last couple of years I have asked my daughter still at home to do this. "Take what you would spend on Dad, place it in a Christmas card, and give it to someone who you feel could really use it. Do this without anyone knowing. It is to be just between you, me, and the Lord." We have had more fun.

I guess the following that someone sent to me really explains how crazy I feel so many things have gone since "the good old days".

During the last couple of years, I have sold thousands of my books at Christmas time for presents. So, this is for you.

A 1990's Politically Correct Christmas!

"Twas the night before Christmas and Santa's a wreck....
How to live in a world that's politically correct?
His workers no longer would answer to "Elves",
"Vertically Challenged" they were calling themselves.

And labor conditions at the North Pole
Were alleged by the union to stifle the soul.
Four reindeer had vanished, without much propriety,
Released to the wilds by the Humane Society.

And equal employment had made it quite clear
That Santa had better not use just reindeer.
 So Dancer and Donner, Comet and Cupid,
Were replaced with 4 pigs, and you know that looks stupid!

The runners had been removed from his sleigh;
The ruts were termed dangerous by the E.P.A.
And people had started to call for the cops
When they heard sled noises on their roof-tops.

Second-hand smoke from his pipe had his workers quite frightened,
His fur trimmed red suit was called "unenlightened."

And to show you the strangeness of life's ebbs and flows,
Rudolf was suing over unauthorized use of his nose
And had gone on Geraldo, in front of the nation,
Demanding millions in over-due compensation.

So, half of the reindeer were gone; and his wife,
Who suddenly said she'd enough of this life,
Joined a self-help group, packed, and left in a whiz,
Demanding from now on her title was Ms.

And as for the gifts, why, he'd ne'er had a notion
That making a choice could cause so much commotion.
Nothing of leather, nothing of fur,
Nothing meant nothing for him, And nothing for her.
Nothing that might be construed to pollute.

Nothing to aim, Nothing to shoot.
Nothing that clammored or made lots of noise.
Nothing for just girls. Or just for the boys.
Nothing that claimed to be gender specific.
Nothing that's warlike or non-pacific.
No candy or sweets...they were bad for the tooth.
Nothing that seemed to embellish a truth.

And fairy tales, while not yet forbidden,
Were like Ken and Barbie, better off hidden.
For they raised the hackles of those psychological
Who claimed the only good gift was one ecological.

No baseball, no football....Someone could get hurt;
Besides, playing sports exposed kids to dirt.
Dolls were said to be sexist, and should be passe;
And Nintendo would rot your entire brain away.

So Santa just stood there, disheveled, perplexed;
He just could not figure out what to do next.
He tried to be merry, tried to be gay,
But you've got to be careful with that word today.

His sack was quite empty, limp to the ground;
Nothing fully acceptable was to be found.
Something special was needed, a gift that he might
Give to all without angering the left or the right.

A gift that would satisfy, with no indecision,
Each group of the people, every religion;
Everyone, everywhere....even you
So here is that gift, it's price beyond worth.....

"May you and your loved ones have our Savior, Jesus Christ, in their
hearts, and enjoy peace on this earth."

Backwoods Glossary A

Up here in the Great North Woods, there is a tendency to use terms or phrases to make a point. To some of you, they may be used in a way you never realized they could be. Other words or terms, you may just have not had the opportunity to ever use. This Backwoods Glossary is to help you out in understanding why we talk like we do.

U.P. (Upper Michigan): If, for some strange reason, you have never traveled in Michigan, these two letters would seem strange to you. First, understand that Michigan has two peninsulas- the upper and lower. The lower peninsula is made up of two parts, Lower Michigan and Northern Michigan. But, the really important part of Michigan lies across the Mackinac Bridge. This part of Michigan is called the U.P., for the Upper peninsula of Michigan. The people up here in the U.P. live in their own little world and like it that way. The only problem is that most of the laws are passed down in Lower Michigan to correct their problems, then they effect us, who may not even be part of that problem. Some of the Big City folks that pass these laws never have learned to understand and love the U.P. like we that live here do. The natives of the U.P. have trouble understanding the "why-for" about some of these laws, therefore they feel they really must not apply to them.

Two of the biggest industries in the U.P. are paper mills and the men that work in the woods suppling trees to these mills so they can produce their product. There are probably more colleges in the U.P., per capita, than anywhere else in the country. But even with this, there are still a lot of natives up here that feel you could sure ruin a good person if you sent them to one of these colleges. News of a serious crime will travel from one side of the U.P. to the other like a wild fire. Because most people up here are not used to it. To them, serious crimes are when someone takes a deer or some fish illegally and is dumb enough to get caught. They don't even take these crimes to seriously unless the poacher should step over the line and get to greedy.

Sports teams that play teams from other towns in the U.P. always seem to have relatives, or friends, on the other team. Everyone knows someone, or someone that married someone, that knew someone from over there. To win a state championship, you have to beat those teams from "down state". To do this is a dream come true for any red-blooded U.P. boy or girl.

When I was growing up, we had only had part-time radios. So we had to be Green Bay (Wisconsin) Packer and Milwaukee Brave fans. As a boy living in the Western U.P., we could not pick up any radio stations that carried broadcast of the teams from Lower Michigan. For this reason, we grew up feeling that we were a state unto ourselves. We could not be part of Michigan, because it was just to far away, and the only way to get there was by boat. We knew we were not part of Wisconsin, so we were just the Good Old U.P.!

Up here in the U.P., where life is tough, but things are good, and it is just a great place to live.

Some backwoods (U.P.) terms:

2-TRACK: (roads)

The U.P. has hundreds of miles of this type of road. All these roads consist of are two tire ruts worn into the ground from all the vehicle travel throughout the years. Usually you have a high, grass-covered center and mud holes in the low spots. This is one of the reasons that so many people in the U.P. feel you cannot live without a 4x4 pickup. These roads are never worked on or improved and you get what you see.

Blacktop Roads:

These are the 2-tracks, that are worse than unimproved roads. They are covered by mud or clay and it is a real trick to stay between the trees on some of these. There are also a lot of these type roads for which the U.P. is famous. Many a fishermen or hunter has spent hours and hours trying to get out of one of these blacktop roads, usually after you misjudged what you were getting into. Two of the first things I learned after becoming a Game Warden stationed in the U.P. were: It's hard to get 2-ton stuck at fifty miles an hour, so wind it up and keep moving. The other one follows point one, you are never really stuck till you stop. In other words, if one of these blacktop areas sneak up on you, floor it and don't stop 'til you reach high ground or hit something unmovable.

Poachers:

These are not people that cook eggs in hot water, but may get themselves in hot water now and then. They are outlaws that rob the honest hunters and fishermen of their chance to get game and fish legally. In years past, it was a way of life in the U.P. that was passed down from generation to generation. When it was an accepted thing to do, the Game Warden not only had a hard time catching the poachers, but he usually had an even harder time trying to get a conviction in the local courts.

Shining:

(Shinning, Shining, Shiners), Shiners are the poachers that use a spotlight to look for deer at night, in order to shoot them. Until the fines got to high, it was the way that a lot of the outlaws did their hunting here in the U.P. They would take a pair of spotlights, hook them up in their vehicle, then drive around while casting the rays of the spotlights out into fields or an old orchards, until they spotted a deer. The deer, blinded by the bright light, would stand there staring at the light while the poacher got out his gun and shot it. There is really no sport in it, because it is so deadly. You will notice I spelled shinning, with two "n's" at times. Well, I did this on my tickets for dozens of cases throughout the years, until a State Trooper told me it was spelled wrong. He said it should only have one "n", so on the next couple tickets I changed how I spelled shining. You see for years, when I caught someone hunting deer at night with a spotlight, the only thing I would write for a charge on the ticket was the one word "shinning". With the one word spelled, Shinning, they knew what they did, I knew what they had done, and most important the average U.P. Judge knew what they were standing before him for doing. Well, the first time I caught a crew out spotlighting for deer and put shining (with one n) on their ticket they pled "Not Guilty". They must have been confused by the spelling and so was I.

Spearers:

These are people that have a way of taking fish with the use of a spear. The spear can have from three to five prongs, with pointed tips, these prongs have barbs on the end to hold the fish on the spear after they spear it. Now in some areas, it is legal to spear certain types of non-game fish. The problem the Game Warden has is with those that spear trout, salmon, walleye, etc. or "game fish". When these fish come into real shallow water to spawn, a Game Warden will spend hour after hour watching the fish spawning in these areas.

Extractors:

This is a term for those illegal fishermen that may come along a creek with a spear trying to extract the spawning fish from the creek. They may use other devices besides a spear. For instance a weighted hook, hand nets, their hands, etc.

Gill Netters:

These are people, both legal and illegal, that use a gill net to take fish. In some areas, there is a commercial fishery allowed with the use of gill nets, but in Michigan it is never legal for "sport" fishermen to use a gill net to take fish. A gill net is made up of nylon string in little squares (it looks something little a small woven wire fence) built so the fish will swim into the net putting their head through the square openings. Then, they get caught when their larger body will not fit through the squares and their gills keep them from backing out of the nets. I have observed illegal gill net fishermen take hundreds of pounds of steelhead in a couple of hours, if they set their gill nets in the right spot.

Fishhouse or fish shed:

In areas of the U.P., along the great lakes where there is a legal commercial fishery, most of those business involved have a building where they clean, box in ice, and store their catch. They may also repair their nets in this building. On account of the smell around a full time commercial fishing operation, most of these sheds are located away from any residence. They also may be on the river bank where the commercial fisherman ties up his fish tug. For this reason they are often used for illegal activity, sometimes by others than those that own them.

Deer camp:

A deer camp can be any type of building used for offering protection from the elements. It is also used to get-a-way from home during the hunting season. Some are as nice as any house, better than some, while others may be made out of plastic, heavy paper, scrap lumber, or anything to keep the weather out. The following rules are some of the usual type that are proper for deer camp life.

(1) You cannot shave or take a bath, no matter how many days you may be staying at camp. You are allowed to wash your face and hands. But this is your own choice, You do not have to if you do not want to. This is one reason young boys love to go to deer camp with Dad.

(2) There is no proper way to dress while at deer camp, if it feels good wear it! You can even wear the same clothes all week long. This includes your socks, if you can catch them after the first three days at camp.

(3) The "menu" is always made up of all the "proper" things that you cannot afford to eat all the rest of the year at home. Both good and bad for you.

(4) It is never wrong to tell a "true" story on another camp member. Remembering it is of more value if you can dress it up a little to make him suffer all the time you are telling it. During the telling of his mis- fortune we must all remember that we will all pay for our mistakes, sooner or later, if and when our hunting "buddies" find out about them.

(5) It is a crime, punishable by banishment, to talk about school, or school work, or any work for that matter while at deer camp.

(6) You can throw, hang or just leave your socks and clothes any where they land when you remove them. You can hang your wet socks from anything that has something to hang them from to try and dry them out before the next days hunt. Always remembering it is "most" important to have dry socks by daybreak the next morning.

(7) What may be called work at home is not work at deer camp. Therefore getting things done at deer camp is not classified as work, but a team effort. For this reason, it is not wrong for a boy to do dishes, sweep a floor, pick up trash (that he missed getting in the trash can when he threw it that way, with one of his famous hook shots), or even do what Dad asks him to do, the first time Dad asks him to do it.

You would have to spend a week at a real U.P. deer camp to really know the true feeling of being a U.P. deer hunter. With these easy-to- apply rules, you can see why deer camp life is so important to a boy during his informative teenage years. It is really important that a young man start out with a proper perspective on life.

Big House:

This is the Michigan State Capital, from some areas of the U.P. it can be over 400 miles away. In Lansing, this is where "they" compile all the rules and ideas that are put out to confuse the average hunter or fisherman, while out in the field. It is the feeling of a lot of U.P. sportsmen, that most of those that work down there, in Lansing's Big House, never in their lives set foot in the real out-of-doors, or wet a line in a back woods stream. What they know, they got from someone that wrote a book without ever having set their feet in a real woods, or having gone back woods fishing either. It is just passed on from desk to desk, year after year, put into volumes of rules and law books that we out in the field have to learn to live with. This while trying to enjoy ourselves out in the real Northwoods, the U.P.

Wifee:

(W-IF-EE; wify) This is one's wife. To pronounce it right, you say the "W" sound, then the "IF", than draw out the "EE".

Big Lake:

This can be any of the Great Lakes that border Michigan. Instead of saying, "I went fishing out on Lake Michigan Saturday". A native from the U.P. would say, "I went fishing on the Big Lake Saturday afternoon".

Off road vehicles:

ATV'S, ORV'S, dirt bikes, etc. These may be any of the type vehicles that are made primary to operate off a improved road. Some may be home made, while other are sold by dealers. In the U.P. you will find a lot of these used by sportsmen to get around when hunting and fishing.

Game Wardens:

Conservation Officer, C.O.'s, and Game Wardens are all one and the same, up here in the U.P. They have been around for better than 100 years serving the people of Michigan. The stories they can tell and those told on them are told over and over around the U.P. This is how my newspaper, story telling got started.

Backwoods Glossary B

Holiday Stations:

Holiday? Here, in Michigan's U.P., you always hear the expression, "I'm going to stop by Holiday on the way". Some of you folks may not understand what a Holiday is and how far advanced the U.P. is over other areas of our country. I'll try to explain. Holiday, here in the north country, is a gas station-store. The Holiday Stations have been around for years and years, and in the U.P. they are like a mini-mall. The U.P. and Holiday were way ahead of the rest of the world on this idea of doing all your shopping in one stop. Get your gas plus whatever else you may need here at Holiday.

Sometimes it just takes awhile for you all to catch up to us, Yoopers.

Years ago, when Christmas time rolled around, you went down to the Holiday to do your Christmas shopping. It had a great toy selection, in fact, in most U.P. towns the best to be found. If company dropped in for a surprise visit and you needed food items, off you went to Holiday to get what you needed. When hunting and fishing season rolled around, they put out a paper and sales ad to get you into Holiday to fill your needs-everything from guns and ammo, to poles, hooks, and line. If you snagged your waders off, you went to Holiday for new ones. If your feet got cold out deer hunting, off to Holiday for warm foot gear. If your motorized deer blind broke down on a weekend, off to the auto parts section of Holiday to get what you needed. What am I saying? Before the rest of the world was smart enough to think about putting other than gas and oil supplies in their gas stations Holiday was there. Now they have moved up one more step because most Holiday Stations have copies of my books for sale.

Remember when traveling through the U.P., if a town does not have a Holiday station, keep on trucking til you find one because that town you are in has not arrived yet!

Copper Country:

In so many parts of my book, you will read about things that took place in the Copper Country. This area covers what is called the Keweenaw

Peninsula over to the area of the copper mines to the west. Those of us that lived in the Copper Country felt you were going into the world of the great unknown if you left Ontonagon, Houghton, Baraga, or Keweenaw County. In fact, a person growing up when I did may have left the Copper Country for the first time when he went into the service. The Copper Country is really a melting pot of people from all over the world. When I was growing up, it was nothing for some of the old folks not being able to speak English; they talked in their native language. In fact, one of the things that really bugged a teenage boy from the Copper Country was when there were a couple of girls your buddy and you wanted to get to know, and they would talk back and forth in Finnish, and we did not have the foggiest idea what they were saying. The history of the Copper Country is both interesting and unreal if you study it. A person could move away and be gone for years, but when asked where they are from, they always answer the Copper Country.

In the Copper Country, everybody knows somebody that knows somebody else. When on a radio show talking about my first book, "A Deer Gets Revenge", a party called in and wanted to know if I was Harry Theiler's grandson. Then another party called in and wanted to know if I was Tim Walker's brother. (Tim is my brother that lives in a home in Hancock, MI, in the Copper Country). Copper Country people are special people that help make up a place called the U.P. where people know and care about each other. Come visit the U.P. and Copper Country someday, and you will see what I mean.

The other day:

I keep telling my kids and the readers of my newpaper article that when I use the saying, "The other day", it could mean anytime between birth and death. It is up to the person you are talking to to try and figure out what era you are talking about. Up here in the U.P., a party could start to tell you a hunting story by saying, " The other day a buddy and I...." and the story may have taken place back in the forties. (1940's) You have to remember that good stories never really get old; they just get better and added to in the telling of them. There was one officer I worked with-could he tell stories! He would get going into a story and you would sit there and listen. Pretty soon bits and pieces would start to ring a bell. Then all of a sudden it would dawn on you that you were with him when "his story" took place, but you really never remembered it happening like he was telling it, or could it have?

One of my boys called me from college a while back (another one of those time means nothing U.P. phrases) to ask me about the history of the 60's. This was for a paper he had to do for a history course. I told him, "Son, the 60's do not qualify as history yet.That is when your dad says, you know the other day, or awhile back, and that makes it today time not history time."

Exspurt:

Sometimes in the U.P. we have our own way of spelling and under-standing things. Here is one of those terms.

I have a buddy that is a U.P. potato farmer. (You have to really wonder about anybody that tries to farm in the U.P.) But this buddy has a great definition for all those exspurts that rule down in the Big House. It is one of those terms you have to think about, but the more you think about it, the more you feel that this potato farmer may go down in histo-ry as a great U.P. philosopher. We will get talking about all those rules and laws the exspurts down in Lansing and Washington pass that are totally unreal, and my buddy will say, "Always remember that an ex-spurt is only a drip under pressure!" Now, I wonder.....

But then,you have all these TV shows on how with an outdoor exspurt on just about everything. Let's be real now. Do they ever get skunked out there fishing? Do you ever see them spending all day baiting hooks for the kids and getting the kids' lines untangled? Or they get the boat unloaded and the motor won't start? Somehow, someway, I get the feel-ing these exspurts have never hunted or fished out there in the real world. Let me give you an example of an exspurt.

One night I happened to be going through the cable channels and came across this exspurt fisherman who had his own TV show. It happened that on this show he was fishing an area off Lake Superior that I was in charge of, so I decided to watch his show. Here is our exspurt telling people how it should be done and where the nice steelhead fishing is in the U.P. As I watched, I couldn't believe it. So I got on the phone and called a Conservation Officer that worked for me and worked the area in the program.

I told him, "John, you blew it and missed one." He repied, "You must be watching the same program I am watching." Then we both had a good laugh. Why? Because here was this exspurt going along a trout stream running out of Lake Superior with an illegal device used to take trout in the spring of the year in that area! I told John, "Maybe we ought to send him a ticket in the mail. We have what he's doing on film, and he is even telling us he's doing it." But you have to understand that this fishing exspurt was a "troll" (a person that lives below the Big Mac Bridge.), and therefore, you get what you pay for. Now, remember what an exspurt is, "A drip under presure", and life will be a lot easier to understand.

Huskavarina edumacation:

There has always been a feeling that there is more wisdom learned at the back end of a chain saw then that you learn in college. The more some of us see and hear what is going on in our country, the more we have to wonder. It was always an amazement to those that worked out in the field for the government to see someone go off to the "Big House" on a promotion and forget everything they learned out in the field in the first six month they were there! In fact, some of us always felt that about halfway down through the lower peninsula there was an invisible force field that made up a brain sucking machine, and by the time they passed through this going to the "Big House", they were useless to us living in the U.P.

We used to suggest that everyone after about a year or two down in Lansing's or Washington's "Big House" ought to have to spend six month back in the woods on the working end of a chain saw to get the feeling for how the real world lives again. That is why the U.P. is a special place, because from the woods, to the mines, to the papers mills, most of its people have a Husavarina Edumacation. Sometimes I think it makes them special people as you can see by some of my stories.

Bugs:

Back when I was a kid, a bug was not an insect. It was something you rode in going hunting. (look at the picture in the books of us hunting in the 40's and 50's, and you will see our Bug.) You would take an old Model T and put oversize tires on it to raise it up off the ground. Then you would find some old tire chains. Most of the time they had no body left on them, and you were to hang on for dear life when you came to a big mud hole. A party always had this saying, "It's hard to get two ton stuck at fifty miles an hour, but when you do you are really stuck." I always said, "You are never stuck till you stop, so the key is never to stop till you hit high ground again." These vehicles were used by all the hunters back before anyone ever heard of a 4x4 pickup. They were homemade, and you were really someone when you had one. In fact I cannot count the times we gave the Game Warden a ride back into the back country when he had something to check on because he was not lucky enough to own a "Bug". But, now if a person was to make one and try to use it, they would end up having to hire a secretary to file the nine thousand-four hundred-seventy-five million tickets you would receive for having this dangerous vehicle back in the woods. Man, those were the good old days; No ORV laws, no snowmobile laws, about half the hunting laws, and no Big Mac bridge to let all those idealists across into God's country.

Yooper:

Have you ever been asked, "What's a Yooper?" It seems that there are certain terms that the real world has not got to use yet. If you take the Upper Penisula of Michigan abbreviated name "The U.P. and sound it out what do you get? It has to be the word Yooper. Therefore all the good people (natives only) that make their homes in the U.P. of Michigan have to be Yooper. Right?

Up here in Yooper Country we have our own jokes, our own Yooper singing groups, our own terms, and a great life style.

The one thing that you want to remember is that you are born a True Yooper. It cannot be bought, you cannot get it by living here for years and years, you must be born a Yooper. We have a real problem with Troles (Those that live below the Big Mac Bridge.) coming up to Yooper land and trying to act like or become one of us, it just cannot be done! You either have it or you don't. You can come see us, we are glad when you spend your money here, we like you for a friend, but remember when you leave Yooper Land you leave as you came, not as a Yooper.

Backwoods Glossary C

The Backwoods Glossary is an ever growing project of backwoods terms. In each new book that comes out, I include the Glossary from previous books and add a new chapter. I have to do this for those that may not have all my books. They just flat need the glossary to help them better understand the stories.

"Bugs":

Back when I was a kid, it was the time before anyone knew what a 4x4 was. If a person in our neck of the woods did know what they were, they sure could never have afforded to buy one. In fact, the only 4x4 you ever heard of was a "Jeep". For this reason a hunter that wanted to get around on the old railroad grades and 2-tracks had to build his own vehicle to do it with. These home-made hunting vehicles were called "Bugs". You would be amazed at what some of the hunters and trappers came up with. Ours was an old Model A with nothing but the frame, windshield, hood, and front seats. The back was a wooden box in which to throw your shovel, chains, and other gear for when you got stuck. And you got stuck in that Ontonagon red clay!! You then put on the biggest size tires you could find that would fit to give you more clearance. After all this was done, you had a hunting "Bug".

I know one guy that could build about anything who had made one up that had chain drive back then. It was really neat to see and would go just about anywhere. You could hardly hurt these "Bugs" because there wasn't enough on them to hurt. One day my dad was coming down the Main Line railroad grade when all of a sudden smoke came pouring out from under the hood! He stopped, jumped off, flipped open the hood and flames came flying out. He grabbed his packsack and beat out the flames. Checking the "Bug" over he found where it had spilled gas, and this caught on fire. After checking it out, he got back on it, started it up and off we drove. There was really nothing to ruin on a "Bug" back then because a vehicle like this only had about a half dozen wires. A "Bug" was really neat and the first vehicle most kids like me ever drove back in those days.

Hunting:

I can still hear my dad telling me, "If you ever become a meat hunter, I'll find you no matter where you are and kick your seat! Always remember that hunting is the time to get away from things and have fun with those you like to be around. If you are lucky enough to get something besides, it is just a bonus."

I have tried to live up to what my dad taught me back then because it would be too hard to walk through the woods hunting while all the time looking over my shoulder watching for dad coming up behind me. I think as you read my tales in my three books you can get my feelings about hunting. Some of the best times we have ever had we came home skunked. Now, don't think we don't like it when we are successful, but we don't build everything on just this. In fact, I am not sure we don't have more fun just before deer season as we scout around looking for deer signs and trying to outwit the deer in figuring out just how they are moving around. Sometimes you guess right, sometimes you don't.

I just wish some of these "exspurt" hunting and fishing shows that are all on cable TV now would show more of the true side of hunting-the days you get skunked, but still had a great time with your buddies. I think the public out there would better understand hunting and the hunter if this were done.

Dad:

I sure wish every boy growing up had a dad like mine. He worked hard at the paper mill, but he always had time for his family. He was not a well-educated person as we would rate education today, but he had more wisdom than almost anybody I have ever met. He was an honest man, and if he said he would do something, you better believe he would do his best to see that it got done. He loved to hunt, but it was the time spent with his boys out there that made it special. One day we were out hunting with Dad. He had to go back to town to attend a union meeting for the mill because at this time he was an officer in the union. He looked at me and said, "I guess it's time for me to resign from the union. When it keeps me away from time with my boys, it's time to give it up." He did. I never really realized till years later what a choice he had made. It was important for him to be a part of the union and to be elected as an officer by his fellow workers. He did not take it lightly. But, his family and his boys were more important even when it hurt. I just hope I have a portion of his values and that I can pass them on to my children as they grow up. I had a great dad and hope you can see it as you read some of my backwoods tales.

U.P.

Learning Curve: I guess that to explain what I am trying to get across in some of my U.P. stories about how the out-of-doors can be used to train up a child to be a good citizen, I could tell this story. It's true, as you go into the main intersection in Ontonagon, you will see a little triangle. On this triangle is a little rock monument with a number of names on it. Some of these are friends that I went to school and played with growing up. These are the names of the residents of Ontonagon County who lost their lives over in Vietnam during the war. I have often sat and thought how lucky I was to be blessed with the life and family I had when theirs was snuffed out at so young an age.

As I recall it so many years later, the news kept coming home to Ontonagon that another boy had lost his life in that land so far away from the backwoods of Ontonagon. As the list grew, some people started to wonder why so high a percentage of those being killed over there were from this little U.P. town of ours. As the list added a few more names, someone finally got hold of people who knew who to contact in Washington to find out what was going on. Some people did some checking, and the answer came back something like this.

"As these boys end up in the service, either by joining or the draft, they seem to have that special quality that makes them end up being trainable. They are the type youth that have pride in what they do, get along with the other service people, and the officers. They end up being where the action is because they are the type people you can depend on. When this happens, and they are where the action is, you have more of them hurt and killed."

I guess we should be proud of the type youth the U.P. turns out even when it hurts as your buddies are sent home for the last time.

Girl Hunters:

There is nothing that can ruin a good hunting camp quicker then having a girl in the group! That was till both my boys were married and moved away and Dad was left with only his baby girl to go out hunting with him. Then, the rules had to change. My girl is an excellent shot and likes to go out. But, a girl will just always be a girl.

We went on a duck hunting trip one day and were jump shooting some ponds. We came to this one where we had to walk back in. It was a warm fall day not made for walking with all your hunting gear on. Cathy went in one side of the lake, and some ducks took off; she dropped one right off. When she shot this duck, the forearm on her shotgun fell apart. The plastic piece that butts up against the metal broke in half. I stuck it back on and told her it should stay.

Some of the ducks had landed on the far side of the lake, so I went all the way around the lake to try and kick them up over her. It was hard, hot going in the water and marsh around the lake. I worked my way to the far side and could not locate the ducks. I continued around the lake to the far end, now sweating like crazy. As I came around the far end and was working my way back to Cathy, I yelled, "Cathy! Can you see the ducks? They have to be over by you!" She stepped out and yelled, "What?" (The normal question that an average teenager asks an adult no matter what they hear."

As she took a step and yelled, the ducks took off from right at her feet!! I figured they were in the blind with her. I yelled, "Shoot!!" But, she never fired a shot. I finally got around to where she was and asked her why she never shot. She showed me her shotgun that had fallen apart again. The forearm was off. I told her, "After all the work I did so you could shoot a duck, you could have at least shot! You can shoot a shotgun without a forearm!" She looked at me and said, "No way, Dad! I watched 911 the other night, and a kid shot a broken shotgun and about killed himself!" What could I say? Girl hunters just think too much.

Smelt:

Anyone who has never been up this way smelt fishing asks me, "What is a smelt?" How do I explain that a smelt is a little silver fish that is from around four to eight inches long? They run into the rivers and streams out of the Great Lakes in big schools to spawn. (There are also some found in inland lakes.) When the smelt runs peak, you will have hundreds and hundreds of people along the Great Lake streams trying to net them. Now, a smelt net is really a handnet. It is a little round net with usually a metal mesh v-shaped basket and a long handle. You dip the net into the schools of smelt and lift them out. It is nothing to fill a 5-gallon bucket with one dip when the smelt runs are in full swing.

A dip net is a net that runs off a pully from a bridge or is operated off a long pole hanging out over the water. They can be up to nine foot square and are operated straight up and down for suckers and smelt. They are real popular in some areas downstate, but not so much so in the U.P.

People catch smelt by the truck loads, and then the fun begins. With smelt, you cook them and eat the bones and all. There is still the need to clean them, and this tends to take all the fun out of smelt fishing. It is nothing to sit five or six hours cleaning smelt steady. The way most people freeze them is to drop them down through the hole in a milk jug, then fill the jug full of water and freeze them in the water. You want to remember, they are best tasting when they are cooked fresh. In fact, when I take kids out smelting, I usually take a coleman stove and cook them right on the beach. They are great then.

Mom's penalty:

You have to remember that there is a down side to everything. The down side to living in an area like the U.P. with all the hunting and fishing is all the junk (all valuable) laying around the house all the time. Remember, sportsmen have to have a different item for each adventure they go off on. Now, Mom is the one who is expected to pick up all this stuff or know where it was placed nine or ten months ago when the fishermen last laid it down. All you women know good and well that a guy cannot be expected to remember where he puts everything to be sure and remember where it is now. I have stored items in a good safe place so I would be sure and find it when I wanted it and have never run across it to this day. But! I can remember picking it up and putting it in a secure place so I would be sure and be able to find it when I needed it again. That is why it is so important to stay on the good side of the lady of the house. You never know when you may need her.

To Order Sgt. Walker's Books

This is the fourth book that Sgt. Walker has published of his humorous backwoods tales. In the first year over 20,000 copies were self-published. They are enjoyed by readers of all ages and walks of life.

The first three books Are:

"A Deer Gets Revenge" ISBN 0-9639798-0-9
These are stories of growing up in the U.P. and true Game Warden Adventures. Crazy, but true. In the first three months the book was out almost 5,000 copies were sold.

"A Bucket of Bones" ISBN 0-9639798-1-7
Some more Game Warden stories and "Yooper" adventures both old and new. This book has a number of colored pictures and old logging pictures. This book sold 2,500 the first month it was out.

"From the Land Where the BIG Fish Live" ISBN 0-9639798-2-5 Back to the old Game Warden tales of the backwoods. More about fishing and trapping in this book. Also some bow and bear tales.

Books can be ordered by sending $10.00 per book, postpaid, to: John A. Walker, 530 Alger Ave. Manistique, MI. 48954. All the books that are ordered from the author are autographed copies.

If you are interested in knowing more about my books, please call me at (906) 341-2082.

My way of saying "Thanks" a Million!

It just amazes me how things have went with my books. From the time my first book came out, and I loaded them in the trunk of my car, and started out to try to sell them, to this day, I stand in amazement at how things have went. Without the help and advice of these listed below and on the following pages, I would still have a trunk load of my first books. I thank them all from the bottom of my heart for just giving me a chance by selling my books.

As you travel around the U.P. and even in "Troll Land" stop in and say "Hi" to some of the greatest people there are.

The Manistique Pioneer Tribune and The Ontonagon Hearld

Canturbury Books, Escanaba and The Book Mart, Kingsford

Flynn's Store, Gulliver and Linda's Bread Box, Cooks

Holiday Helpers, Nordin's Foods, and Ken's Fairway, Manistique

Dukes Sport Shop, Comfort Inn, and Rahilly's IGA, Newberry

Golden Grill, Seney, Eagle's Nest, Germfast, & Curtis IGA

Sandy's Gifts, Wilderness Sports, and The Historical Museum, Ontonagon

The IGA in Harvey and Marquette. Wolverine Sports, Escanaba

Wilderness Sports and Buck's Restaurants, Ishpeming

Jack's, Rapid River and DeLon's Restaurant, Gladstone, Hardee's Manistique

Bronner's Christmas Wonderland, Frankenmuth, Jay's Sports, Clare and Bass Pro Shop, Springfield, Mo.

Also, Buck LeVasseur of Discovering, Ken and Al on the radio in Escanaba and Jan Tucker's program from Ontonagon. Plus, all the "real" outdoor writers who were kind enough to tell their readers about my books.

I Could sure use your help.

I guess one of the first things I was to find out after writing my first book, "A Deer Gets Revenge", was how hard it is to get the information out about your book.

There are those authors that have a natural audience because of who they are or who they may write articles for. Then there are those that write for a little out of the main-stream newspaper. When you fall into this category like I do the self-publishing book business is a real project.

In some areas the people were really helpful with an unknown author from the middle of nowhere. While in other areas I had no luck at all getting the local news outlets to let people know about my books. There was really no rhyme or reason to what took place and the author has really no control over things.

I thought I would let you know about this need and ask for your help. If, you enjoyed the books and should know someone in your area that could help get the news out about them, please let them know about the four books.

I guess one of the greatest things to come out of writing the books, has been the doors that have been opened to speak to groups. I have spoken at church banquets, senior citizen dinners, colleges, and a number of other groups about my books. I sure enjoy doing this.

End of the line